Shaker
Band Saw
Project

Shaker Band Saw Projects

Mark Duginske
& Chris Morris

Sterling Publishing Co., Inc.
New York

This book is dedicated to the memory of
Edward Duginske 1912–1992
Doris Morris 1915–1992
Dennis Duginske 1940–1994

Drawings by Chris Morris and Jenny
Wilcox

Library of Congress Cataloging-in-Publication Data

Duginske, Mark.
   Shaker band saw projects / by Mark Duginske & Chris Morris.
      p. cm.
   Includes index.
   ISBN 0-8069-8248-9
   1. Band saws. 2. Woodwork. 3. Furniture, Shaker. I. Morris,
Chris, 1972–   . II. Title.
TT186.D853   1994
684'.083—dc20   94-16846
                                                              CIP

10 9 8 7 6 5 4 3 2 1

Published by Sterling Publishing Company, Inc.
387 Park Avenue South, New York, N.Y. 10016
© 1994 by Mark Duginske and Chris Morris
Distributed in Canada by Sterling Publishing
% Canadian Manda Group, One Atlantic Avenue, Suite 105
Toronto, Ontario, Canada M6K 3E7
Distributed in Great Britain and Europe by Cassell PLC
Villiers House, 41/47 Strand, London WC2N 5JE, England
Distributed in Australia by Capricorn Link (Australia) Pty Ltd.
P.O. Box 6651, Baulkham Hills, Business Centre, NSW 2153, Australia
Printed and bound in Hong Kong
All rights reserved

Sterling ISBN 0-8069-8248-9

CONTENTS

Introduction

ANYONE LOOKING THROUGH woodworking or furniture magazines or project books will notice that Shaker furniture and woodworking projects are extremely popular. There are reasons for this popularity. Shaker works, which consist of circular elements and gentle curves, are simple, yet elegant. They are also practical and utilitarian. A Shaker project can complement and serve a purpose in any room.

The band saw is the tool of choice for making Shaker projects because it can be used to make traditional joinery such as tenons and dovetails, which are featured in Shaker projects. In the following pages, I describe and illustrate how to use the band saw to create dozens of Shaker works. Included is a chapter on one essential part of band-saw use: tuning it. The band saw is like a musical instrument, and needs to be adjusted for maximum performance. A properly tuned band saw becomes more important the more complex the project. If you are interested in learning more about the band saw, refer to my books *Band Saw Handbook* and *Band Saw Basics* (Sterling Publishing Company).

The projects in this book range in complexity from simple ones such as hanging shelves, wood boxes, and quilting stands to benches, step stools, tables, chairs, and projects in which steam-bending techniques are used. Easy-to-understand patterns are supplied with virtually all of the projects. (See Chapter 4 for information on using patterns.) Because many of the projects are small, if a mistake is made not much wood is wasted. Also, shrinking the size of a project can often save it, if a mistake is made near the edge of a board.

I think you will discover in the following pages a wide range of intriguing Shaker projects. Hopefully, this book will provide you with hours of pleasure and, along the way, some family heirlooms.

Mark Duginske

CHAPTER 1

The Shakers

RALPH WALDO EMERSON could have been speaking about the Shakers when he said, "We ascribe beauty to that which is simple, which has no superfluous parts, which exactly answers its ends." Those of you who have had the good fortune to visit a Shaker community, view a Shaker collection, or examine the many books containing Shaker history and artifacts will certainly feel that Emerson might have been referring in part to those items crafted by Shakers. A sense of order and tranquility sweeps over a person as he or she experiences the simple beauty of these items. It is certainly true, as said by June Sprigg, the noted Shaker authority, that "we in the world miss a lot of what it means to be Shaker." Yet, the spirit of the Shakers shines through in their designs and crafts, and people caught up in today's hectic pace respond to these qualities. After battling the stresses of modern-day life, opening a door leading into a room filled with Shaker design pieces will prove very therapeutic.

Almost every issue of any current home-decorating magazine has rooms or objects

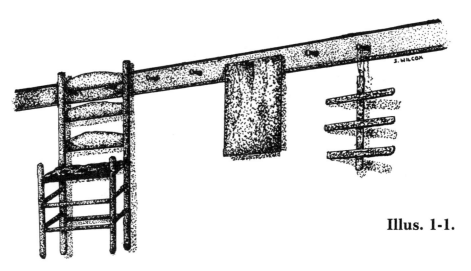

Illus. 1-1.

in Shaker-like styles. Most major furniture companies also feature Shaker-like pieces; these companies recognize that such designs do not dominate or overpower other styles of furniture. Shaker designs are also popular with furniture makers and manufacturers today for some of the same reasons they was popular with the Shakers: They are uncomplicated, practical, versatile, and simple to make.

"Mother" Ann Lee, the founder of the United Society of Believers in Christ's Second Appearing, emigrated from England to America in 1744. She was attracted in 1758 to a religious sect of Shaking Quakers led by James and Jane Wardley. This sect believed, among other things, that the Second Coming of Christ would be in the form of a woman and that a confession of one's innermost sins was essential to salvation.

Ann Lee was at the forefront in establishing what were eventually known as the Shaker communities. Originally, the name Shaker was used as a term of derision to mock the worshippers' ecstatic movements during religious services, but eventually the term was taken and used by the Shakers themselves.

Shaker furniture was made by artisans who lived within these religious communities, where they were inspired by the belief that their love of God should be expressed in their workmanship. The religious society of the Shakers eventually became communal; living, working, and worshipping in large communities led to a tremendous outpouring of productivity, in part because the Shakers felt that it was their God-given duty to teach honest trades.

The Shakers should not be confused with the Amish. The Shakers were never hesitant to adopt new technology and used electricity, telephones, and automobiles. Their inventiveness directed towards better time management saw the development of a washing machine, circular saw, flat broom, and the common clothespin, to name but a few inventions.

The Shakers practised equality among the sexes and races, common ownership of property, celibacy, and pacifism. They also spoke out in favor of the abolition of slavery and in support of child welfare, women's suffrage, and compulsory education laws. They believed that their mission on earth was to use their time and talents in the manner that they might be most useful. Inscribed on a Shaker memorial, erected in 1816, is the following: "Therefore our labor is to do good, in our day and generation, to all men, as far as we are able, by faithfulness and frugality in the works of our hands."

As people joined the Shaker religious societies, they often gave those communities their land. Many Shaker sites were often built in difficult locations, and the innovative Shakers adapted these sites to their purposes. The same innovativeness can be seen in the Shakers' woodworking designs. At the apex of the growth of the Shaker communities—18 sites scattered from Maine to Florida—there was a pressing need for furnishings to supply them. These furnishings had to be produced inexpensively with unskilled labor. Simple but elegant designs were developed that could be produced rapidly but uniformly from one community to another, as directed from the parent ministry in New Lebanon, New York. Shaker designs had to be, first and foremost, useful and soundly constructed. Perfection of workmanship, not beauty, was desired. Extra adornment was to be avoided, but, nevertheless, it was from this exquisite "less-is-more" style that the beauty emerged. All objects made by the Shakers were to be given the same quality of workmanship.

Therefore, not only the most public of places but the most common objects such as the inside of a closet door show the same standard of perfection.

According to Edward Deming Andrews, who wrote *Religion in Wood: A Book of Shaker Furniture*, the first book popularizing Shaker furniture, this approach to crafting simple, high-quality items characterized Shaker craftsmanship. He noted that "their chairs used no more wood than needed, slats that could have been made straight across but gently curve instead, rungs that ever so slightly taper, posts that soar." Long dining tables, work counters, and benches were some of the more common types of furniture produced in the Shaker society. The wood most often used for furniture such as cupboards, boxes, benches, and tables was pine, which was available in wide diameters on the various Shaker properties. Special pieces such as

Illus. 1-2. *Some of the Shaker projects featured in the following pages.*

sewing tables and writing desks were made from cherry, maple, or mixed woods. Ash, hickory, and white oak were used for bent parts, and apple and pear wood were used for drawer pulls.

Completed pieces of furniture were given either a coat of paint in any of a variety of shades from browns to blues to yellows or were covered with a stain, shellac, or a varnish that allowed the grain of the wood to shine through. Both veneering and grain painting were avoided, because this was seen as deceptive.

While the Shakers produced many objects to sell to the public, ranging from packaged seeds to blankets to produce, the only furniture specifically made for sale to "the world" or those outside of their own society was the chair. The most skillful woodworkers set the tone of excellence that we now associate with Shaker work. Stylistic differences were evident between the furniture made in eastern Shaker villages and the furniture made in the Ohio and Kentucky communities. One factor that contributed to this difference was simply the geographical distance between the parent ministry and the western communities. This distance allowed for a greater form of self-expression in design. Western Shaker furniture has often been referred to as the "poorer cousin" of eastern Shaker furniture. But many people today are looking at western Shaker furniture differently, and are recognizing the unique strength of its plain country style.

The classic period of Shaker furniture started in the 1820s and ended around 1860. According to John Kassay in his *Book of Shaker Furniture,* the pieces produced during this time were expressions of utility, simplicity, and perfection attributable to spiritual inspiration rather than a conscious effort to create the timeless masterpieces that we now consider them to be. But as the agrarian communities began to enter the industrial age, Shaker membership began to decline and communities began to close. With the exception of chairs, only a small amount of furniture was produced after the American Civil War.

Highly publicized auctions and private sales over recent years indicate the tremendous amounts of money people will spend to acquire authentic Shaker pieces. Despite the exclusivity this has created, the general public has become perhaps even more familiar with the Shakers and has developed an appreciation of their lifestyle and accomplishments. Likewise, we hope the information contained in the following pages will lead you to better appreciate and understand their craftsmanship.

CHAPTER 2

Tuning Up and Adjusting a Band Saw

IN ORDER FOR the band saw to operate at its optimum level, it has to be properly tuned and adjusted. This includes tracking and tensioning the blades, adjusting the thrust-bearing guides and guide posts, and aligning the wheels. Each of these aspects is described in the section below.

Having a well-tuned and -adjusted band saw in your shop has many benefits. It will greatly increase your confidence and your cutting options. It makes the work more efficient and enjoyable. With a well-tuned band saw, you can rip small pieces that are dangerous to cut on table or radial arm saws. There is no danger that they will kick back with a band saw. If a well-tuned band saw can help prevent an accident, all the attention you give it is certainly worth the effort.

BLADE TRACKING

Every time you put a new or different blade on the saw, you have to track it. The term "tracking" refers to the act of posi-

tioning or balancing the band-saw blade on the wheels. There is no external force that holds the blade on the wheel. It is held on by a combination of two factors. One factor is the outside shape of the wheel. The second is the angle of the top wheel. Both are discussed below.

Wheel Shape

The shape of the wheel is determined by the shape of the metal casting on the rim of the wheel. The outside rim of the wheel is covered with a piece of rubber, called a *tire,* which is between ⅛ and ¼ inch thick. The tire acts as a cushion and a shock absorber. It also protects the blade from contacting the metal wheel, and thus from causing damage to the teeth.

Wheels either have a crown or flat shape (Illus. 2-1). The crown exerts a controlling force on the blade which causes it to ride near but not exactly in the middle of the wheel. A flat wheel is designed so that the operator can track the blade either in the middle of the wheel or towards the

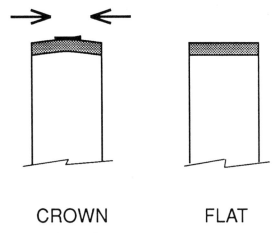

CROWN   FLAT

Illus. 2-1. *The crown exerts a controlling force which helps track the blade near the middle of the wheel.*

front of the wheel. Both systems have advantages and disadvantages.

The disadvantage of a crowned wheel is that it provides less surface area between the blade and the tire. This makes it more difficult to track large blades such as a ½-inch blade, which is the best blade to use for straight cuts, especially for resawing. Another disadvantage is if the wheels are not perfectly aligned with each other, the crowns on each wheel will compete for control of the blade. This causes vibration and shortens the life of a blade.

A flat wheel provides good support for wide blades, but you have to be more careful when tracking the blade. With a flat wheel, you can track the blade in various positions on the wheel. Wide blades are best tracked towards the front of the tire. Narrow blades are best tracked towards the middle of the tire.

The main disadvantage of a flat wheel is that when the tire starts to wear, a depression forms in the tire and makes the blades harder to track. You can alleviate this by dressing the tires with sandpaper so that there is a crown of about .020 inch, or the thickness of five pieces of paper.

Top-Wheel Angle

The second factor that affects the tracking of a blade is the angle of the top wheel. The angle of the top wheel steers the blade in the direction of the tilt (Illus. 2-2). The usual approach is to tilt the top wheel, usu-

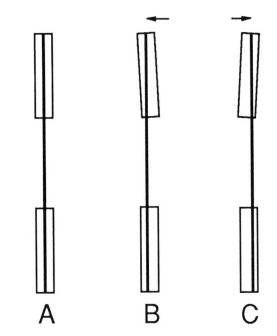

A   B   C

Illus. 2-2. *The angle of the top wheel steers the blade in the direction of the tilt.*

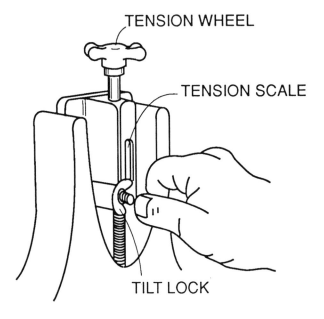

TENSION WHEEL

TENSION SCALE

TILT LOCK

Illus. 2-3. *Tilting the top wheel.*

ally rearwards, until the blade tracks in the middle of the top wheel (Illus. 2-3). This approach is the one that is usually recommended in the owner's manual. It is called *center tracking* (Illus. 2-4).

Center tracking works well on blades that are ³⁄₁₆ inch wide or narrower. These blades are flexible, and the misalignment of the wheel doesn't harm their performance or their life expectancy. However, larger blades—those wider than ¼ inch—are not flexible like the narrower ones. Track these wider blades with the wheels lined up with each other, rather than with the top wheel angled. This is called *coplanar tracking* because the wheels are in a coplanar position (lying in the same plane) (Illus. 2-5).

When tracking wide blades, your goal is to allow the blade to run as straight as possible. If the wheels are coplanar, the blade will find its own equilibrium and essentially track itself. With coplanar tracking, the blade exerts the same amount of pressure on the tires at all points of contact.

Illus. 2-4. *Use center tracking (A) on blades that are ³⁄₁₆ inch wide or narrower. Use coplaner tracking (B) on blades that are ¼ inch wide or wider.*

Illus. 2-5. *Coplaner wheels lie in the same plane.*

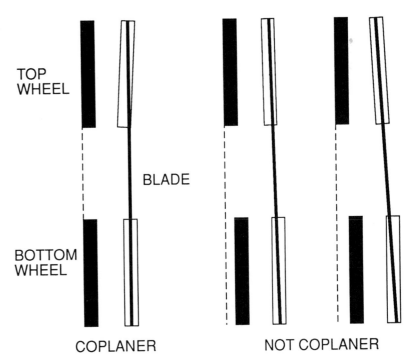

TOP WHEEL

BOTTOM WHEEL

BLADE

COPLANER   NOT COPLANER

There is no binding, which occurs when you angle the top wheel. The blade will last longer and cut straighter, and will require less tension for good performance.

One of the things that you will notice when you are using coplanar tracking is that the blade will have a tendency to track towards the front of the wheels. The reason why this area is the position of equilibrium is that the front of the blade is shorter than its back. When the blade is manufactured, the teeth are first ground and then hardened, which causes the front of the blade to shrink in relationship to the back. The difference between the front and the back is greater on wide blades.

Tracking Procedure

Many people do not like to change saw blades, and go to great lengths to avoid doing it. However, to use the band saw to its greatest advantage, you will have to use the appropriate blade and quickly change and track it—a habit that can be easily developed if you are so inclined. If you use a consistent step-by-step method, tracking should take only a minute or two.

Be careful when using blades, especially wide and sharp ones. Some people prefer to use gloves when handling large blades. Safety glasses are always a good idea. Following are the step-by-step procedures for tracking a blade:

Removing the Blade

1. Unplug the saw.
2. Remove the mechanism for aligning the table halves. It will be a pin, a bolt, or a front rail.
3. Unscrew the blade guard or open the hinge.
4. Remove the throat plate.

5. Release the tension, thus lowering the top wheel.
6. Expose the wheels by opening or removing the covers.
7. Take the blade off the wheels with both hands, and carefully slide it out of the table slot.
8. Fold the blade.
9. Retract the thrust bearings above and below the table.
10. Loosen the guides on the side of the blade and then retract them also. This way, you can easily install the next blade without having any obstructions.

Installing the Blade

1. Uncoil the blade. Remember to use gloves and safety glasses. If it is a new blade, it may have oil or dirt on it. The blade may have been oiled to prevent rust. You do not want the oil or dirt touching the workpiece, so remove it before installing the blade. Wipe it off with a rag or a paper towel. Pull the blade through the rag rearwards so that the teeth don't catch on the rag.
2. Hold the blade up to the saw. Inspect the teeth. If the teeth are pointed in the wrong direction, you will have to turn the blade inside out. To do this, hold the blade with both hands and rotate it.
3. Hold the blade with both hands, the edges of its teeth towards you. Slide it through the table slot and place it on the wheels. Some people like to handle it from the top wheel, because then they are taking advantage of the force of gravity.
4. Position the blade where you want it on the wheels. Then tension it (make it taut between the wheels). Use the tension knob to slowly raise the top wheel. Start to rotate the wheels by hand in the normal direction while the blade is still fairly slack. As you do this, watch to determine where

the blade wants to track. If the blade is tracking too far forward or rearwards, make an adjustment with the tilt mechanism. As you rotate the blade with one hand, increase its tension, or tautness, with the other. Continue to do this until you have adequate tension. A blade cannot be correctly tracked until the tensioning is completed. Never track the blade with the saw running.

5. After the blade has been tracked, replace the cover and the blade guard. Plug in the electrical cord. Turn the saw on for a second, and then turn it off again. Watch to see how the saw runs. If the blade seems to track well, run it at full power. Below are the specific tracking instructions.

Center-Tracking Instructions

If you are using *center tracking* (best for ⅟₁₆- to ¼-inch blades), rotate the wheel by

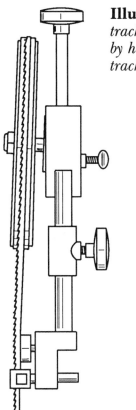

Illus. 2-6. *When center-tracking, rotate the top wheel by hand until the blade tracks in the middle of it.*

hand and angle the top wheel until the blade is tracking in the middle of the top wheel (Illus. 2-6). Make several revolutions of the blade to ensure that the blade stays in the same place on the wheels. Lock the tilt knob. Center tracking works best on blades that are ³⁄₁₆ inch wide and narrower.

Coplanar-Tracking Instructions

If you are using *coplanar tracking*, align the wheels with a straightedge (Illus. 2-7). Make several revolutions of the blade to make sure that it stays in the same place on the wheels. The blade may or may not track in the middle of the top wheel. The blade will usually track towards the front of the wheels. Lock the tilt knob. Tilt the

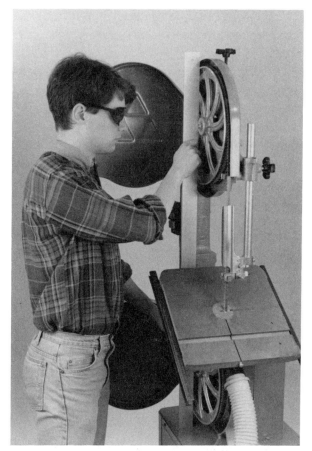

Illus. 2-7. *The first step in coplaner tracking is aligning the wheels with a straightedge.*

top wheel slightly rearwards if the blade starts to move forward or comes off the front of the saw. Coplanar tracking works best with blades that are ¼ inch wide and wider.

ADJUSTING THE BAND SAW

There are certain parts of the band saw that have to be adjusted so that the saw can make accurate cuts. Before you learn to adjust them, you should be aware of how they function.

As the workpiece is moved into the blade, a mechanism is needed to prevent the blade from being shoved off the wheels. On most saws, a round wheel bearing called the *thrust bearing* is used to stop the rearward movement of the blade (Illus. 2-8). There are usually two thrust bearings: one above and one below the table.

Guides are paired with each thrust bearing on each side of the blade. The guides prevent the sideways movements, or deflection, of the blade. They also prevent excessive twisting of the blade when it is being used to cut curves. There are usually four guides, one on each side of the blade above and below the table.

The guides and bearing are held in place by a metal casting called the *guide assembly*. There are two guide assemblies: one above and one below the table (Illus. 2-9). The top guide assembly is attached to the guide post, which is movable up and down and is thus adjustable to the thickness of the workpiece.

Each guide assembly has a mechanism for the independent forward-and-rearward movement of the guides and the thrust bearing. This guide-assembly design accommodates different blade widths.

Adjusting the Guide Post

As mentioned, the top guide assembly is attached to a movable post that is raised or lowered to accommodate different thicknesses of wood. The post should be adjusted so that there is about ¼ inch of clearance between the bottom of the post and the top of the workpiece (Illus. 2-10).

To get a good performance out of the band saw, it is important that the two thrust bearings support the blade equally. This means that the top and bottom thrust bearings must be aligned with each other. Unfortunately, the guide post does not always go straight up and down, which would maintain the alignment of the bearings. For this reason, it is best to adjust the height of the post *before* adjusting the

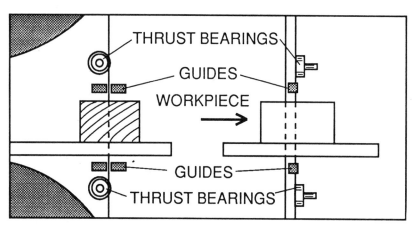

FRONT VIEW   SIDE VIEW

Illus. 2-8. *The thrust bearing is located behind the blade and prevents the blade from being shoved rearwards by the workpiece. The guides are located on each side of the blade, and prevent twisting and deflecting.*

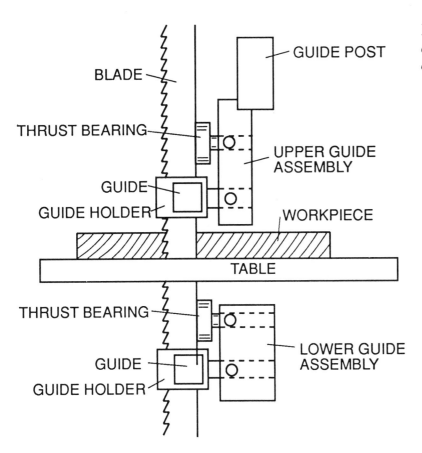

GUIDE POST

BLADE

THRUST BEARING

UPPER GUIDE ASSEMBLY

GUIDE

GUIDE HOLDER

WORKPIECE

TABLE

THRUST BEARING

LOWER GUIDE ASSEMBLY

GUIDE

GUIDE HOLDER

Illus. 2-9. *The guide assembly is a casting that holds the bearings and the guide holder.*

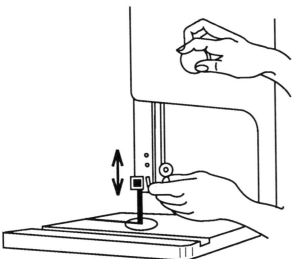

Illus. 2-10. *The guide post is adjustable up and down.*

thrust bearing and the top guide blocks. You should recheck the top thrust bearing and the top guide blocks for alignment each time you raise or lower the post.

Squaring the Table

It is also important that the blade and table be square to each other. Check and readjust the table before adjusting the thrust bearing and the guides. Use a high-quality square for this procedure. Check the squareness frequently.

Adjusting the Thrust Bearings

The next step is to adjust the thrust bearings. Position the blade weld opposite the bearings. The blade is being used as a straightedge, and the weld is the least straight part of the blade.

Position the two thrust bearings about 1/64 inch (0.15 inch) behind the blade (Illus. 2-11). When the cut begins, the blade moves rearwards and contacts the thrust bearings. When the cutting stops, the blade should move forward again, and the bearings should stop rotating. You can use a feeler gauge or a dollar bill folded twice to determine the correct space between the blade and the bearings.

Adjusting the Guide Blocks

Next, adjust the guide blocks. As mentioned, the four guide blocks are held in place by the guide holders that are paired with each thrust bearing above and below the table. Some manufacturers use bearings instead of solid-metal guides. In recent years, a nonmetal replacement guide block called Cool Blocks has become very popular. Cool Blocks are a patented fibre with a dry lubricant that greatly decreases the friction between the blade and the blocks. This decreases the heat generated by the blade and thus increases the life of the blade.

Another advantage is that the Cool Blocks can be placed in contact with the blade. This decreases twist and deflection, and improves the accuracy of the band-saw cut.

Place the metal guide blocks about .004 inch away from the blade. This is the thickness of a piece of paper, so you can use a dollar bill as a spacer. You must be careful when doing this. The distance between the gullet and the front of the guide block should be about ⅟₆₄ inch because the blade will flex rearwards during the cut (Illus. 2-11).

ROUNDING THE BLADE BACK

One step that improves blade performance and blade life is to round the back of the blade with a stone. A round blade back creates smooth interaction between the thrust bearing and the blade. If the blade rotates slightly, there is no sharp blade corner to dig into the thrust bearing. Also, the rounding process smooths the

BEFORE CUT   AFTER CUT

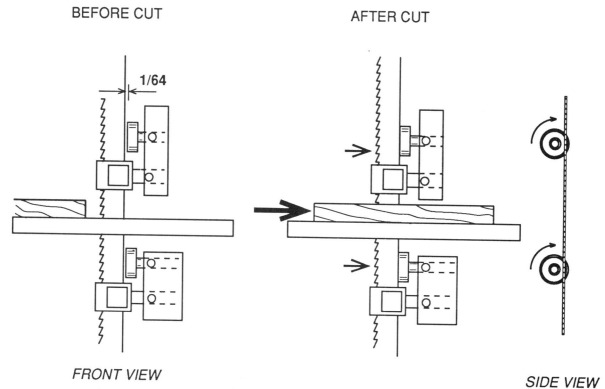

FRONT VIEW   SIDE VIEW

Illus. 2-11. *The blade should not touch the thrust bearings unless the saw is cutting.*

weld. A blade with a round back makes tight turns better because the round back has smooth interaction with the saw kerf.

After the guides have been adjusted, hold the sharpening stone against the corner of the blade for about a minute. *Wear safety glasses when rounding the blade.* Then do the same thing on the opposite corner.

Next, slowly move the stone to round the back of the blade. The more pressure you put on the back, the faster you will remove the metal. Be careful that the inside of the machine is free of sawdust, because sparks could start a fire.

On small blades such as a ⅛- or 1/16-inch blade, the pressure on the back of the blade may bring the blade forward off the front of the wheels. To prevent this, it is best to feed wood into the blade during the rounding process (Illus. 2-12). Pass the wood underneath the elevated stone. This keeps the blade in contact with the thrust bearing.

USING NARROW BLADES

Until recently, the narrowest blade that was available for the band saw was ⅛ inch wide. The latest development for band saws is a blade that is only 1/16 inch wide. This blade makes extremely tight turns, similar to those made by an expensive scroll-saw blade.

A band saw that can make very tight turns has an advantage over a scroll saw in that it can cut much faster, especially in thick, hard stock. That is why the 1/16-inch blade is becoming very popular, even with those who already have a scroll saw.

To use the smaller blades successfully, you will have to make some changes in the standard adjustment procedure. It is necessary to replace the metal guides. Cool Blocks seem to work best. Place these blocks just behind the gullets (Illus. 2-13).

As mentioned in the previous section, you should round the back of a narrow band-saw blade. Also, use center tracking to track the blade. Keep the top guide assembly about an inch above the work. This will allow the blade to flex rearwards slightly during the cut. This eliminates the possibility that the blade will be forced to make a sharp angle under the top thrust bearing. The thrust bearing should rest against the back of the blade with no space

Illus. 2-12. *Feed the wood into a ⅛- or 1/16-inch-wide blade while rounding the blade with a stone.*

Illus. 2-13. *This band saw is fitted with ¹⁄₁₆-inch blade and Cool Blocks. Cool Blocks are replacement guide blocks that allow the use of small blades and prolong normal blade life.*

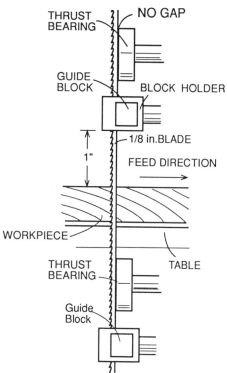

Illus. 2-14. *You can extend the life of narrow blades if you follow a few simple rules. When using a narrow blade such as a ¹⁄₈- or ¹⁄₁₆-inch blade, keep the top guide about an inch above the workpiece. This will allow the blade to flex rearwards slightly during the cut. Cool Blocks should be used because with these blade guides there is less destructive blade heat generated. This is especially important with small blades because there is less metal to act as a heat conductor. The cooler the blade, the longer it will last.*

between the bearing and the blade. This gives the small blades added support.

A ¹⁄₈- and ¹⁄₁₆-inch blade last significantly longer when the guide is raised. However, this exposes about an inch of blade, which could be a potential hazard, *so use extra caution* (lllus. 2-14).

ALIGNING BAND-SAW WHEELS

Aligning band-saw wheels is a very simple procedure that should take only a couple of minutes to accomplish. The wheels may or may not be already aligned, so first check to determine if they are. Use the following steps to check, and then to align the band-saw wheels:

1. *Tension the blade.* Tension the widest blade that you can use on your saw. Tensioning is stretching the blade taut between the wheels. The ½-inch blade is the largest practical size to use on a consumer band saw. Use the tension scale on your band saw.

2. *Make sure that the wheels are parallel to each other.* With a straightedge, check to determine if the wheels are parallel with each other. You may have to angle the top wheel to get them parallel.

Put the straightedge in the middle of the wheels. If it touches the top and bottom of both wheels, then the wheels are parallel and in line—they are coplanar (Illus. 2-15). If this is the case, you do not have to align them.

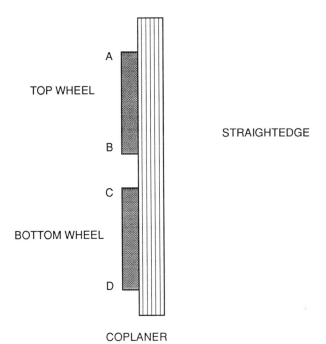

Illus. 2-15. *The wheels are coplaner if the straightedge touches the tops and bottoms of both wheels. These positions are designated in the drawings as A, B, C, and D.*

If the wheels are not in alignment, the straightedge will not touch the top and bottom of both wheel points (Illus. 2-16). Instead, it will either touch the top and bottom of the top wheel or the top and bottom of the lower wheel. In either case, you will have to move one of the wheels to make both wheels coplanar.

3. *Measure the misalignment.* It is important to know how far one of the wheels has to be moved to achieve coplanar alignment. This is essential if you are going to achieve coplanar alignment by adding or removing washers from behind the wheels.

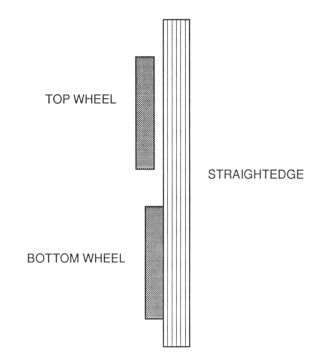

Illus. 2-16. *If the wheels are not coplaner, the straightedge will only touch one wheel.*

Measure the misalignment at the top and bottom of the wheel that is not touching the straightedge. The measurements at both points should be the same. If they are not exactly the same, angle the wheel until they are. Once they are the same, that amount is the distance the wheel needs to move to align the wheels (Illus. 2-17). In the situation shown in Illus. 2-18–2-20, the amount of misalignment in the top wheel is being measured.

4. *Make the adjustment.* On Sears and Inca models, the adjustment is made with a movable bottom wheel. This is the easiest and most convenient way. The bottom wheel is mounted on a shaft in a keyway (a groove on the shaft that prevents the wheel from spinning on the shaft), and the wheel is locked in place with a setscrew. When making the adjustment, loosen the screw and move the wheel the desired amount.

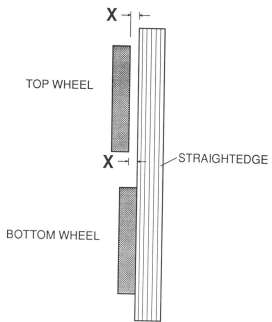

TOP WHEEL

STRAIGHTEDGE

X

BOTTOM WHEEL

Illus. 2-17. *It is important to know how much to move the wheel to make the wheels coplaner. Measure this amount from the top and bottom of the wheel that is not touching the straightedge.*

Illus. 2-18. *Hold the straightedge against the bottom wheel.*

Illus. 2-19. *With a straightedge against the bottom wheel, use a ruler to measure the distance between the top wheel and the straightedge. You may have to hold the straightedge against the bottom wheel with your knee.*

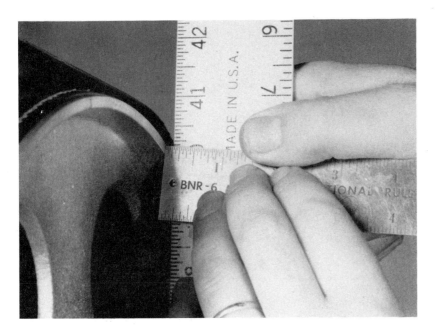

Illus. 2-20. *With a fine ruler, make the final measurement.*

On the Delta and Taiwanese band saws, the adjustment is made on the top wheel, which is mounted on a threaded shaft and held secure with a nut. To make the adjustment, unscrew the nut and then remove the wheels; this will expose the washers. Make the alignment by either adding or removing washers. You can buy additional washers at hardware dealers.

After the first alignment, always rotate the wheels several times to make sure that the blade is tracking; then recheck the alignment.

Make a habit of realigning the wheels often. Think of the procedure as just another adjustment that should be made. After you have aligned the wheels a couple of times, it will become very simple to do. And you'll notice how useful it is—the minute that it takes for alignment is a small price to pay for good performance.

CHAPTER 3

Maintenance, Troubleshooting, and Safety Techniques

MAINTENANCE PROCEDURES

There are three main parts of the band saw that require maintenance: the wheel tires, the thrust bearings, and the guide blocks. The tires are made of rubber, and wear just as a car tire does. They wear in the middle, which causes a concavity in the tire. This is especially true of tires that are flat. The concavity makes it hard to track the blade.

For this reason, it is important to maintain the original shape of the tires. This can be done by sanding the wheel with 100-grit sandpaper. To do this, first remove the blade. Never sand the tires with the blade on the machine. Sand the bottom tire with the saw running (Illus. 3-1).

To rotate the top wheel, use a drill with a sanding drum that is about 1½ inches in diameter (Illus. 3-2). You may feel more comfortable sanding the bottom tire if you use sandpaper attached to a stick (Illus. 3-3).

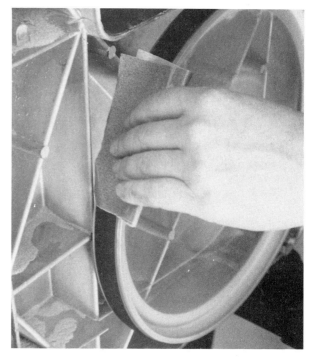

Illus. 3-1. *The wheel tires should be cleaned and their original shapes restored occasionally. Here, medium-grit sandpaper is being used to clean and shape the bottom tire while the saw is running.*

Illus. 3-2. *The top wheel does not have a source of power, so an outside source such as a drill can be used to rotate the wheel. Here a drill with a 1¼-inch-diameter sanding drum is being used to rotate the wheel.*

Illus. 3-3. *You may feel more comfortable sanding the band-saw wheel if the sandpaper is mounted on a stick.*

Thrust bearings can wear or become scarred. Some of these bearings can be removed from the shaft and reversed, thus providing a new surface. Check the rotation of the bearings frequently. If the bearings do not rotate easily, they should be replaced. Order the new bearings from your dealer or the manufacturer.

Guide blocks can also wear and can become rounded. Cool Blocks wear slightly faster than the metal guides. Both types of blocks should be resurfaced as needed. Resurface the blocks with a file or a power disc or a belt sander.

DIAGNOSING PROBLEMS

There are a number of problems that band-saw users may encounter. These include blade breakage, crooked cuts, and vibration. There are different reasons for these problems. Following is a list of problems, the reasons for them, and solutions:

Blade Breakage
REASON
A. Excessively high feed rate.
B. Guides or bearings are poorly adjusted.
C. Blade tension is too high.
D. Band is too thick in relationship to the diameter of the wheels and the sawing speed.
E. Poor weld.
SOLUTION
A. Slow the feed rate.
B. Readjust the guides and bearings. (See Chapter 2.)
C. Decrease the blade tension. Use only as much tension as you need to perform an operation.
D. Use a narrower band.
E. Replace blade.

Crooked Sawing
REASON
A. Guides and bearings are poorly adjusted.

B. Blade tension is too low.
C. Dull blade.
D. Pitch is too fine.
E. Damaged teeth.
F. Fence is poorly aligned.
SOLUTION
A. Readjust bearings and guides properly. (See Chapter 2.)
B. Increase the blade tension to the recommended amount.
C. Have blade sharpened or replace blade.
D. Use blade with coarser pitch (fewer teeth per inch).
E. Replace blade.
F. Realign fence.

Excessive Machine Vibration
REASON
A. Stand or bench is on uneven floor.
B. Machine is not mounted securely to stand.
C. Poor-quality drive belt.
D. Belt not tensioned correctly.
E. Bent or poor-quality pulley.
F. Motor not fastened securely.
G. Eccentric wheels.
SOLUTION
A. Reposition on flat surface. Support low end with a wedge. Fasten to the floor if necessary.
B. Tighten all mounting bolts using lock washers.
C. Replace belt.
D. Readjust tension.
E. Replace with high-quality cast and machined pulley.
F. Tighten all bolts.
G. Isolate motor and saw with rubber pads, preferably shock-absorbing pads.

SAFETY PROCEDURES

The band saw is a popular tool because it is easy to use and because it is so versatile. It is also fairly safe to use. However, you should not assume that because you are using a band saw, accidents are not possible. *Read the following safety rules carefully, and observe each and every one.*

1. Read and understand the instruction manual that comes with the saw before operating it.

2. If you are still not thoroughly familiar with the operation of the band saw, get advice from a qualified person.

3. Make sure that the machine is properly grounded, and that the wiring codes are followed.

4. Do not operate the band saw while under the influence of drugs, alcohol, medication, or if tired.

5. Always wear eye protection (safety glasses or a face shield) and hearing protection (Illus. 3-4 and 3-5).

6. Wear a dust mask (Illus. 3-6). Long-term exposure to the fine dust created by the band saw is not healthful.

7. Remove your tie, rings, watch, and all jewelry. Roll up your sleeves. You do not want anything to get caught in the saw.

8. Make sure that the guards are in place, and use them at all times. The guards protect you from coming into contact with the blade.

9. Make sure that the saw-blade teeth point downwards towards the table.

10. Adjust the upper blade guard so that

Illus. 3-4. Eye and hearing protection (Illus. 3-5) should always be worn while woodworking.

it is about ¼ inch above the material being cut.

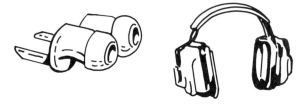

Illus. 3-5. *Hearing protection.*

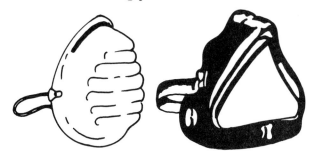

Illus. 3-6. *Fine dust is a potential health hazard, so wear a dust mask.*

Illus. 3-7. *A push stick should be used at the end of a cut.*

11. Make sure that the blade has been properly tensioned and tracked.

12. Stop the machine before removing the scrap pieces from the table.

13. Always keep your hands and fingers away from the blade.

14. Make sure that you use the proper size and type of blade.

15. Use a push stick at the end of a cut (Illus. 3-7). This is the most dangerous time, because the cut is complete and the blade is exposed. Push sticks are commercially available, but can also be shop-made.

16. Hold the wood firmly and feed it into the blade at a moderate speed.

17. Turn off the machine if you have to back the material out of an uncompleted or jammed cut.

CHAPTER 4

Using Patterns

A PATTERN IS THE shape of the desired item that you plan on making. It can be drawn directly on the workpiece or it can be drawn or copied on a piece of paper which is then attached to the workpiece. The paper can be taped in place or it can be attached with an adhesive such as rubber cement (Illus. 4-1).

TYPES OF PATTERN

Full Pattern

The full pattern is used when the shape of the object is not symmetrical (that is, its proportions are not balanced). It is impor-

tant to consider the direction of the wood's grain when laying out a pattern on the piece of wood. Illus 4-2 shows the full pattern of a horse. The wood's grain runs the length of the pattern. The two weakest areas are the tops of the two middle legs because the pattern runs *across* the grain rather than *with* the grain. These areas are the places that are most likely to break. In a situation where there are a lot of weak areas, consider using plywood. Plywood is very strong when used in narrow sections.

Half-Pattern

When the object is symmetrical, a half-pattern is the best pattern to use. A half-

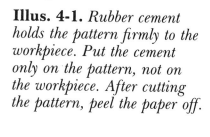

Illus. 4-1. *Rubber cement holds the pattern firmly to the workpiece. Put the cement only on the pattern, not on the workpiece. After cutting the pattern, peel the paper off.*

pattern is only half of the shape. You can use the same pattern for both sides of the object by drawing one side and then flip- ping the pattern over and drawing the other. A simple example would be the pattern shown in Illus. 4-3.

Illus. 4-2. *The grain of the wood runs along the length of the pattern.*

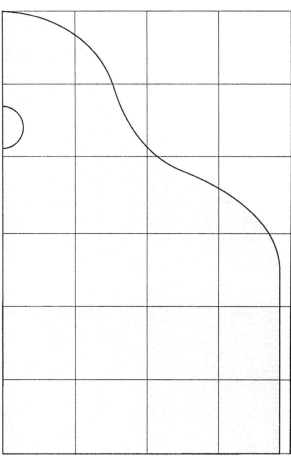

Illus. 4-3. *This half-pattern represents half of a hanging shelf.*

CHAPTER 5

Simple Projects

THE SHAKERS DEVISED a system for keeping their dwellings orderly and to conserve space. This system consisted of boards mounted on the wall with pegs from which objects could be hung. The pegs were used to hang clothes, candle sconces, clocks, mirrors, and chairs. Most small objects that the Shakers made had holes that were used to either hang them from the pegs or in which to place strings that could be used to support the object from pegs.

The projects in this chapter (Illus. 5-11– 5-29) are simple in design and fairly easy to make. As with all projects, think the process through before you cut the wood. Some of these projects are designed to be hung from the wall. There are three options for hanging projects, as shown in Illus. 5-1. A board can have a number of pegs, with the entire board attached to the wall. Another option is to attach a small board with one or two pegs that is screwed directly into the wall. A third option is to use single pegs with a metal screw that are screwed into the wall; these are now available from some of the woodworking supply catalogues. It's advisable to screw the

Illus 5-1. *Many Shaker objects were designed either to hang from pegs or hang from a string. Shaker rooms have a board around the room with pegs, as shown at the top of this photo. A short board can also be used, as shown on the left. A recent development is a peg that can be screwed into a wall, as shown on the right.*

peg or the board into a stud, if possible.

Before making the projects in this chapter, read the information under the heads Half-Circle Jig and Radius Cuts. This information will help you to make circle and corner cuts more easily and efficiently.

HALF-CIRCLE JIG

Many projects require partial circles. Shop-made jigs prove helpful in cutting partial circles. There are several methods for cutting circles with a jig. The first consists of advancing the jig and the workpiece into the blade. An easier method consists of clamping the circle-cutting jig to the table and only rotating the workpiece into the blade.

Another way to cut a partial circle is to make a jig that holds the workpiece. This jig will rest on top of the circle-cutting jig. Then rotate the jig and the workpiece together. Illus. 5-2–5-4 show such a jig: one used to cut half-circles. This jig is a piece of plywood with a rotation point on the bottom of it. Two plywood sides are added to stabilize the workpiece. A clamp is used to hold the workpiece in place during the saw cut.

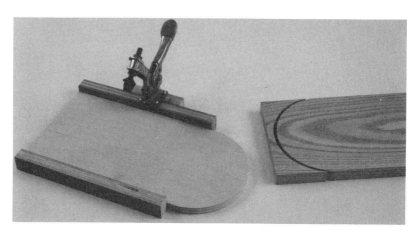

Illus. 5-2. *The half-circle jig consists of a piece of plywood with strips of plywood nailed to its sides. An adjustable clamp is used to hold the workpiece during the saw cut.*

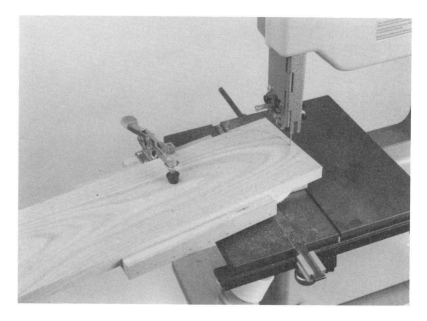

Illus. 5-3. *The half-circle jig rests on top of the circle-cutting jig. This circle-cutting jig, a commercial jig that is manufactured by INCA, cannot be shown here. The cut shown here is half completed.*

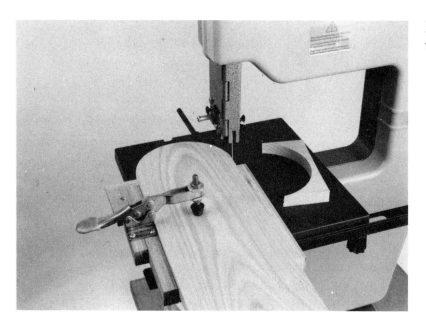

Making a Half-Circle Jig

To make a half-circle jig, do the following:

1. Cut a piece of plywood that is the diameter of the circle.
2. Make a hole for the rotation point. The hole should be half the width of the plywood (which is the radius of the circle).
3. Using the rotation point, make the half-circle cut in the plywood.
4. Attach two sides to the plywood base. This will keep the workpieces stable during the cut. You can also add a clamp to secure the workpiece to the jig.

RADIUS CUTS

When a corner cut is made, thus forming a quarter-circle, it is referred to as a "radius" cut. To make a radius cut, mark off the piece so that the middle of the circle is the same distance (radius) from the edge of the board all along the edge (Illus. 5-5). Position the workpiece on the circle-cutting jig.

Mark the center or rotation point by making two equal measurements, one from each edge of the board. Illus. 5-6 shows the center point being marked. Use an awl to mark the point and to make a hole. Move the jig nail or point to the proper distance from the blade, which is the same measurement as the radius. Place the workpiece hole over the jig point and make the cut (Illus. 5-7).

Illus. 5-5. *A quarter-circle cut is usually referred to as a radius cut.*

Illus. 5-6. *Mark the center, or rotation point, by measuring an equal distance from each edge of the board. In this case, the rotation point is an inch from the edge.*

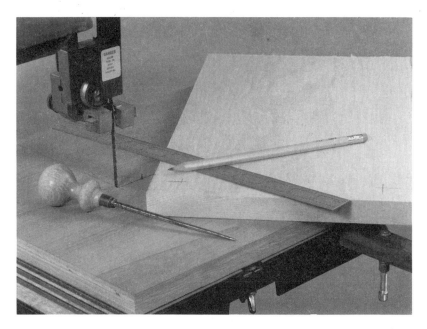

Illus. 5-7. *Rotate the piece into the saw blade, thus making a quarter-circle cut with a half-inch radius.*

Radius Jigs

If multiple pieces are to be made, you can easily make a radius jig by attaching two strips of wood to each side of a complete piece (Illus. 5-8). This will prevent the effort of having to mark, punch, and locate each corner. Simply hold the workpiece against the jig sides and rotate the jig (Illus. 5-9 and 5-10). It is important that the circle-cutting jig does not move during this operation, and for this reason you may

Illus. 5-8. *You can make a radius jig by adding a wood strip to each side of a complete piece.*

Illus. 5-9. *Hold the workpiece in the corner of the jig and make the cut.*

Illus. 5-10. *You can make the cut without having to measure, mark, or make a hole.*

want to clamp it to the table. You can also use this jig in conjunction with a sanding belt to sand the corners. By placing the wood sides away from the smooth corner, you could finish the cut with a flush-trimming bit on a router table.

PROJECTS

Illus. 5-11–5-29 contain plans and details for simple Shaker projects. These consist of hanging shelves, candle sconces, wood boxes, and quilt racks.

Illus. 5-11. *The Shakers made a large number of hanging shelves. This pipe-box design is from Sabbath Day Lake, Maine. This example is in cherry, but a variety of woods were used by the Shakers. It is suspended from a peg by a leather string. It could also be attached directly to the wall. This is an example which may require some resawing because some of the material is only ¼ inch thick. This is a good project for the pattern-sawing technique that ensures that both sides of the piece are exactly the same shape; this technique is described in Chapter 4.*

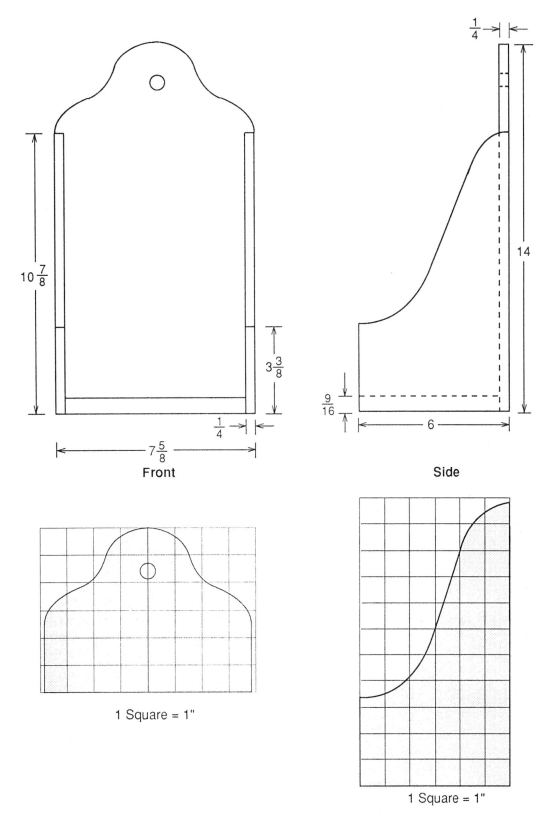

Illus. 5-12. *Plans for the hanging shelf shown in Illus. 5-11.*

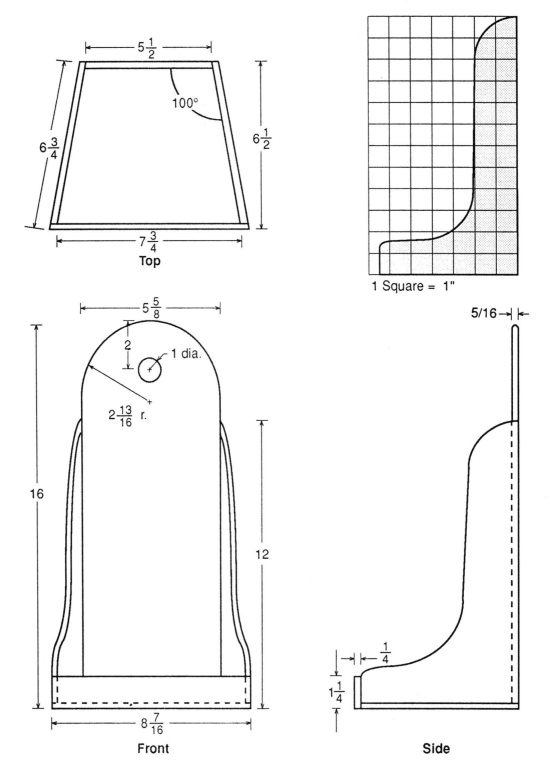

Illus. 5-13. *Plans for the half-circle hanging shelf shown in Illus. 5-14.*

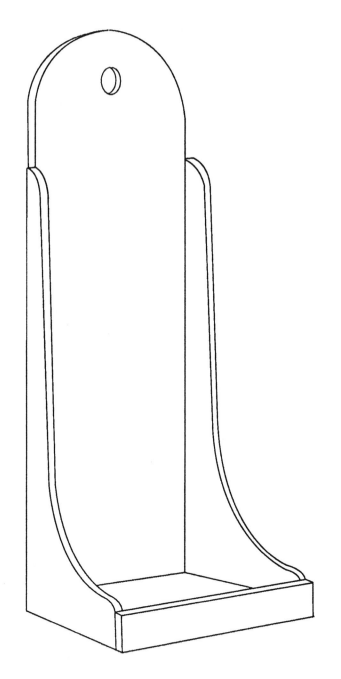

Illus. 5-14 (left). *Hanging shelf with half-circle. This drawing is of a candle sconce that was made in the New Lebanon, New York, community in the first quarter of the 19th century. The original is made from butternut and stained orange. This is a very delicate project, and the material is quite thin. This is another good project for resawing. Because the top consists of a half-circle, this would be a good project for using a half-circle jig if you have a number of these to make.*

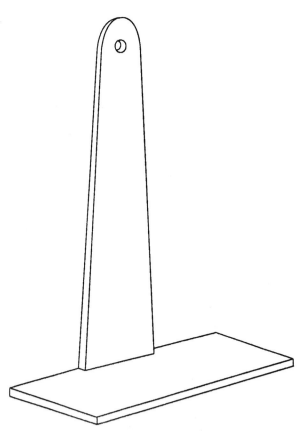

Illus. 5-15. *This hanging shelf was originally designed as a twin candle sconce at the Shaker community in Hancock Shaker Village in Pittsfield, Massachusetts. It's an extremely simple design. This is a good project for using a taper jig (see Chapter 8) and it's also a good project for a radius circle jig (pages 33 and 34). The material is thin, so it's a good opportunity to do some resawing also.*

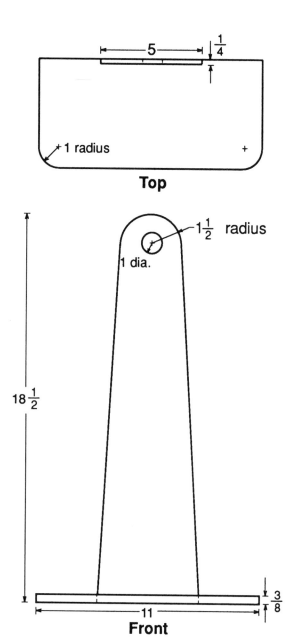

Top

Front

Illus. 5-16. *Plan for the twin-candle sconce hanging shelf shown in Illus. 5-15.*

Illus. 5-17. *This is a large candle sconce. It is actually more complex than it first appears. The top semi-circular element can be made on the band saw using the circle-cutting jig, and the bottom board can be made using a radius jig.*

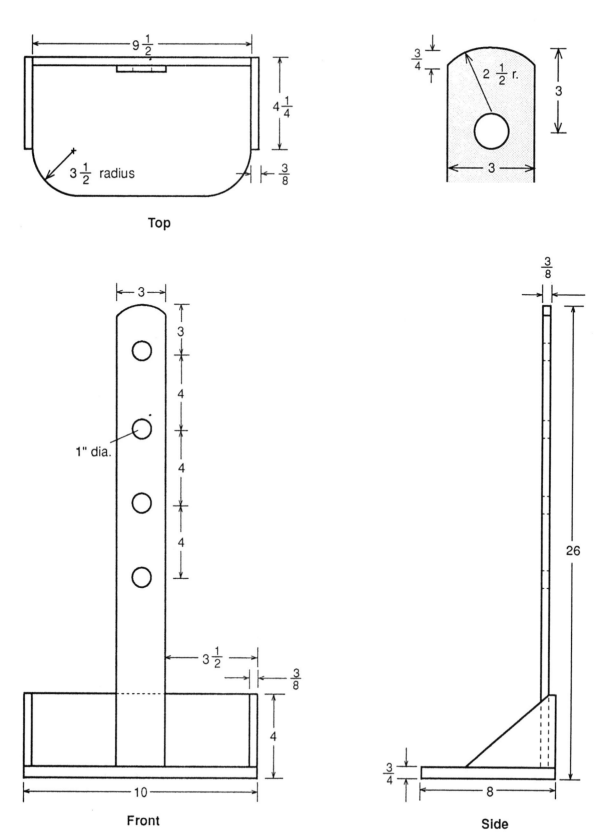

Illus. 5-18. *Plan for the large candle sconce shown in Illus. 5-17.*

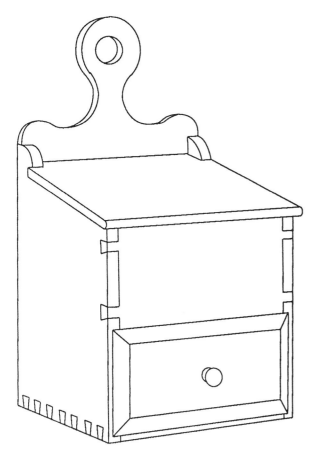

Illus. 5-19. *This utility box was made in the mid-19th century at the Union Village in Ohio. The backboard is composed of three different-sized circles: 2¹⁄₈, 2¹⁄₂, and 2³⁄₄ inches. These can be marked out with a compass or a drafting-circle template. It may be advisable to make the curves with a drill bit in a drill press if you have a 2¹⁄₂-inch drill bit. The bottoms of the sides are dovetail joints; if you don't feel comfortable with dovetail joinery, an option is to make a solid bottom that is wider than the sides. For further information on making dovetails, see the* Band Saw Handbook. *See Illus. 5-21 for the plans for making this utility box.*

Illus. 5-20. *This hanging shelf is typical of many of the hanging shelves that the Shakers used. These shelves were used both in living quarters and in the utility areas such as kitchens and other work areas. It's a good idea to do all the joinery such as making the dado before you actually cut the curves for the shelves. This is a good project for the taper jig described in Chapter 8. See Illus. 5-22 on page 42 for the plans for making this hanging shelf.*

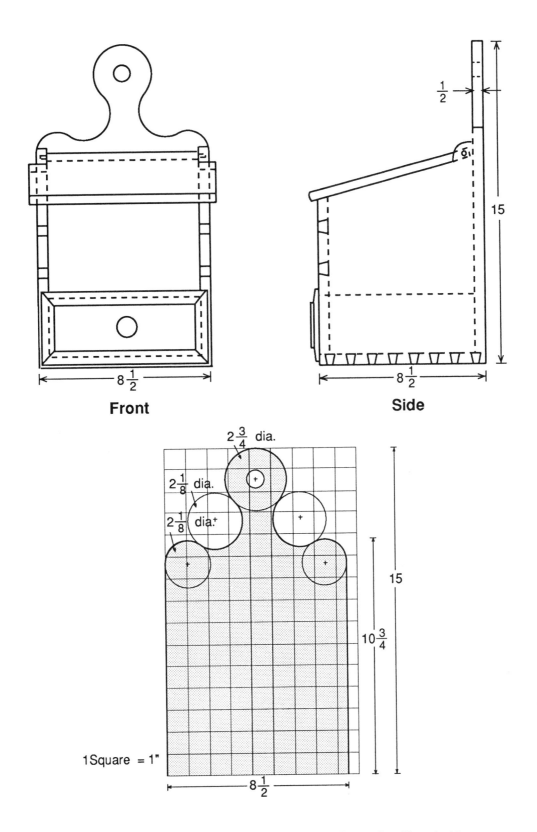

Front

Side

$2\frac{3}{4}$ dia.

$2\frac{1}{8}$ dia.

$2\frac{1}{8}$ dia.

$\frac{1}{2}$

15

15

$10\frac{3}{4}$

$8\frac{1}{2}$

$8\frac{1}{2}$

$8\frac{1}{2}$

1 Square = 1"

Illus. 5-21. *Plan for the hanging utility box shown in Illus. 5-19.*

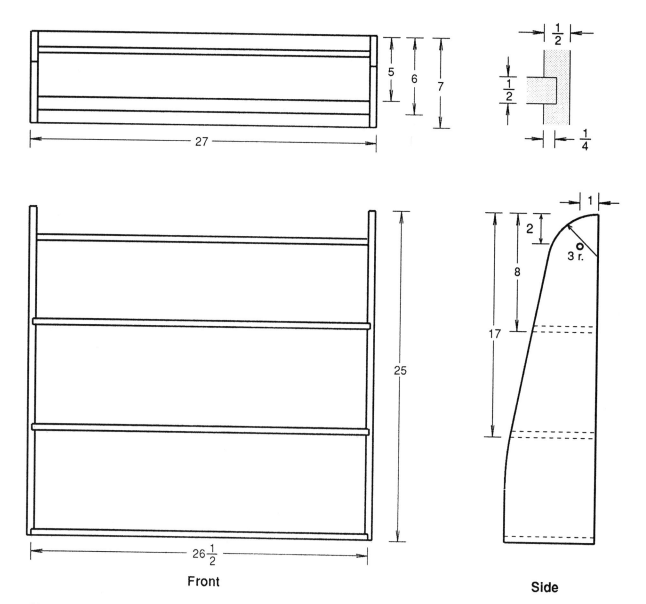

Front

Side

Illus. 5-22. *Plan for the hanging shelves shown in Illus. 5-20.*

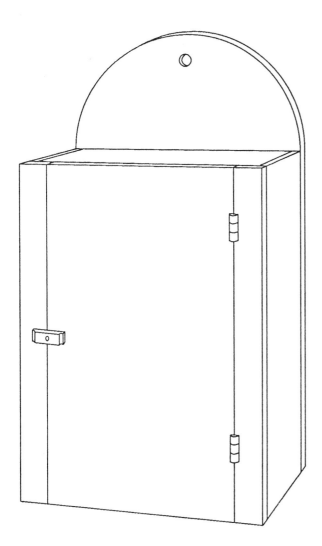

Illus. 5-23. *This hanging shelf is actually a small box and was designed to hang from one of the Shaker pegs. It has a door, so the object inside the cabinet could be hidden. Theoretically, the sides could be dovetailed to the top and bottom, but that would make the project much more complex. It would be acceptable to attach the two sides to the top and bottom with a rabbet joint. The top is semi-circular, so this is a good project on which to use a circle-cutting jig. The door stiles are nailed in place, and a little "keeper" secures the door. See Illus. 5-25 on page 44 for the plans for making this hanging shelf.*

Illus. 5-24. *The Shakers used a number of racks for drying herbs, clothing, and towels. Today, a rack is a good way to store or display quilts or weavings. This design features two cross-bars that are mortised into the upright, which is also mortised into the curved base. (Refer to the information in Chapter 8 on making a tenon on the band saw.) You have the option of using a through or a blind tenon. The Shakers used both. The racks were made with a number of different types of woods and were either painted or stained. See Illus. 5-26 on page 45 for the plans for making the rack.*

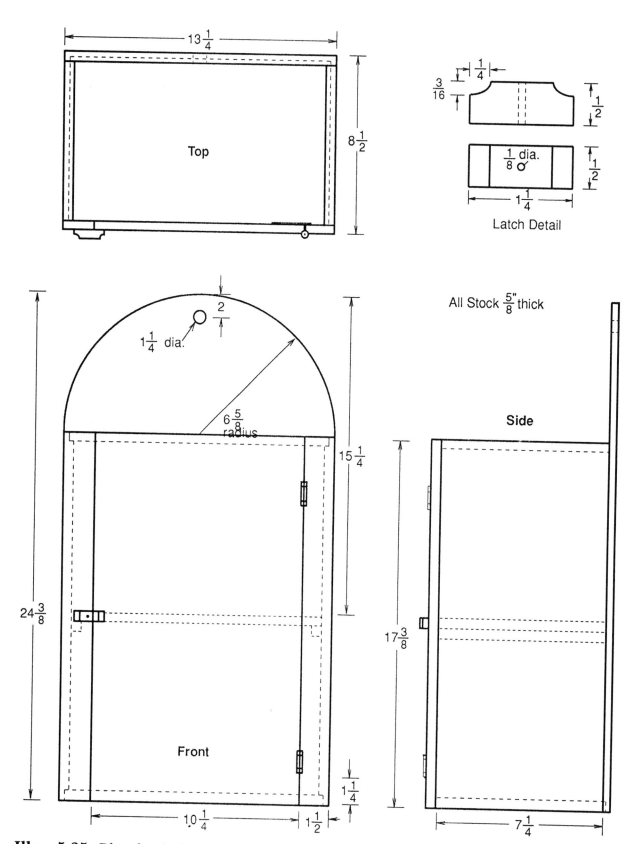

Illus. 5-25. *Plan for the hanging shelf or cabinet shown in Illus. 5-23.*

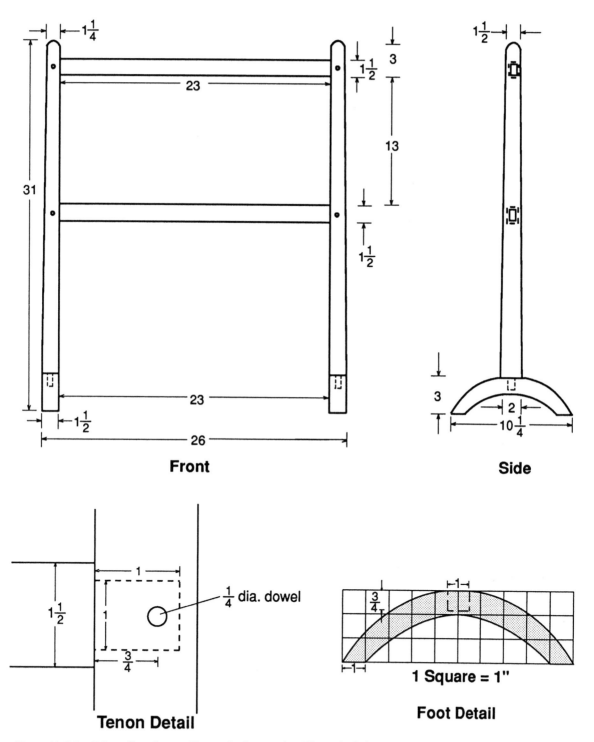

Front

Side

Tenon Detail

$\frac{1}{4}$ dia. dowel

Foot Detail

1 Square = 1"

Illus. 5-26. *Plan for the quilt rack shown in Illus. 5-24.*

Illus. 5-27. *This wood box is modelled after one made in the Pleasant Hill, Kentucky, Shaker community. It is made of poplar. The original is painted red. This box is an example of the western style of Shaker craftsmanship, which is different from the rigid designs of the east. Although the original was made from one very wide poplar board, the pieces for this wood box will have to be glued together. It may be a good idea to cut the curves on the two side pieces and put the seam where the two curves meet towards the back of the sides. The front is fastened to the sides with wood screws or nails.*

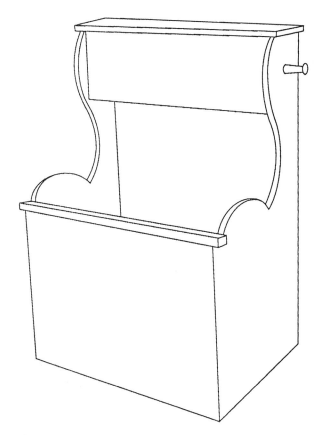

Illus. 5-28. *Pattern for the wood-box side.*

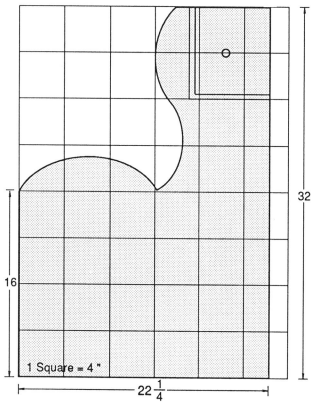

1 Square = 4 "

32

16

22 $\frac{1}{4}$

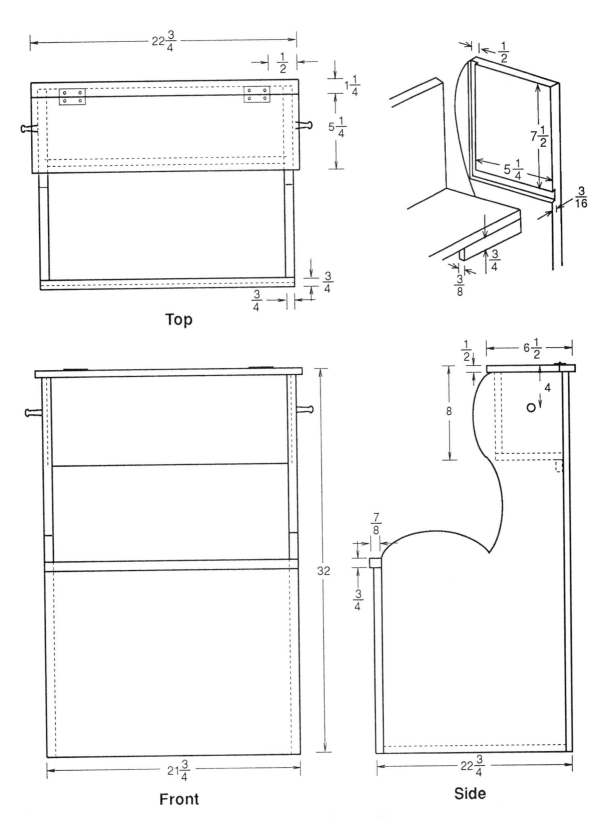

Top

Front

Side

Illus. 5-29. *Plan for the wood box shown in Illus. 5-27.*

CHAPTER 6

Benches

THE SHAKERS MADE a variety of benches. Most of their benches were originally made for sitting, but the designs for these benches can be used for a number of different purposes in the modern home. Some of the smaller ones can be used to make tables. Many incorporate semi-circular patterns. If the benches are going to be sat upon, it's advisable to increase the length of the legs to 17 or 18 inches.

The construction methods for these benches range from simple nailing and screwing to more complex joinery, as will be used on the bench shown in Illus. 6-1. The bench in Illus. 6-7 can be nailed or screwed together, or it can be put together with a more complicated through-tenon as shown in Illus. 6-8.

Illus. 6-1. The Shakers made a number of small benches that had semi-circular design elements. The easiest way to make this bench is to make the ends from two different pieces, make the semi-circular cut on both pieces, and then glue them together. This particular Shaker bench was made at Hancock Village in Pittsfield, Massachusetts.

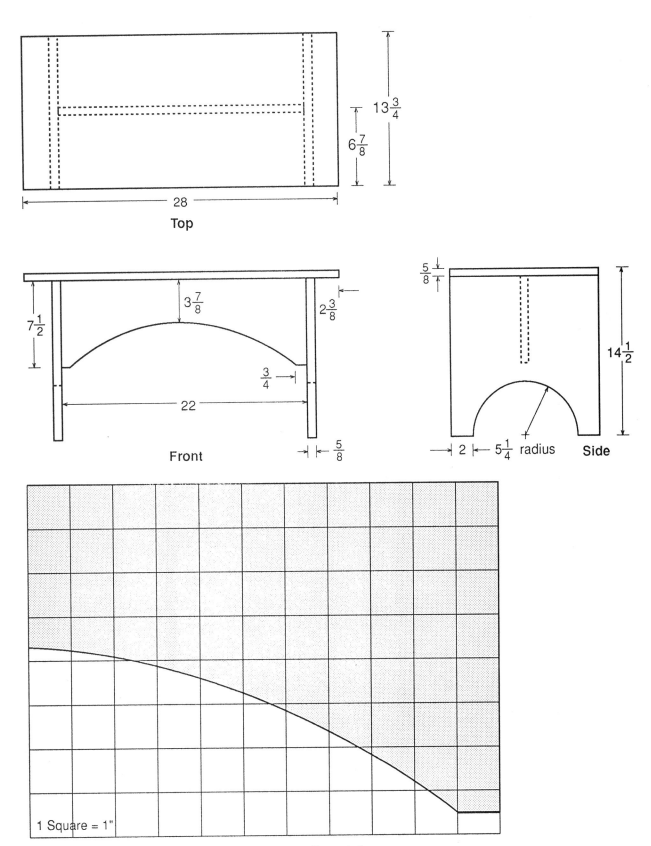

Illus. 6-2. *Plan for small bench shown in Illus. 6-1.*

Illus. 6-3. *A close-up of a circle-cutting jig composed of an aluminum extrusion dadoed into a piece of plywood. The point slides in the extrusion and is locked in place with an allen key.*

Illus. 6-4. *The workpiece is positioned over the point, which is located between the blade and the column. With this arrangement, the workpiece doesn't rotate into the column.*

Illus. 6-5. *This small bench is made of cherry and is from Pleasant Hill, Kentucky. The western Shakers made a number of interesting furniture pieces that were not made in other communities. When building this bench, make the sides and top first. The top is fitted to the sides with a dado. Then make the cross-members. The cross-members are screwed into the ends.*

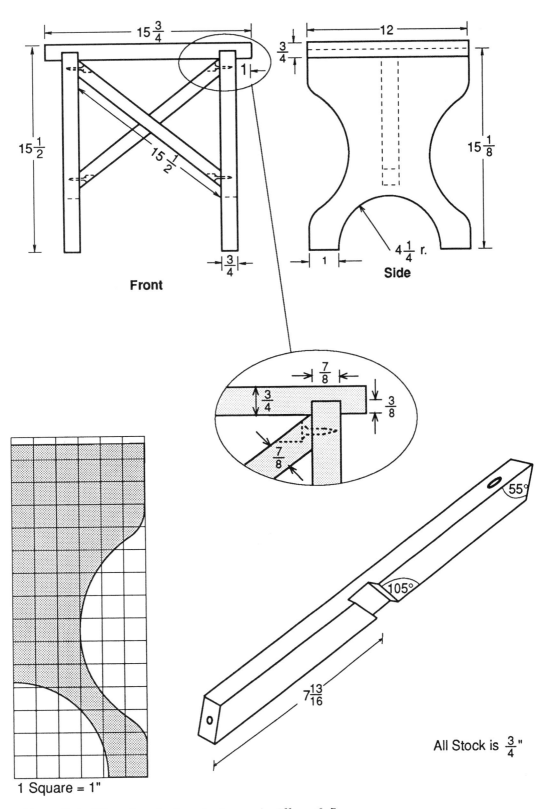

Illus. 6-6. *Plan for the bench shown in Illus. 6-5.*

Illus. 6-7. *This Shaker bench was made at the South Union Community during the first half of the 19th century. The Shakers made large numbers of benches similar to this for their meeting halls.*

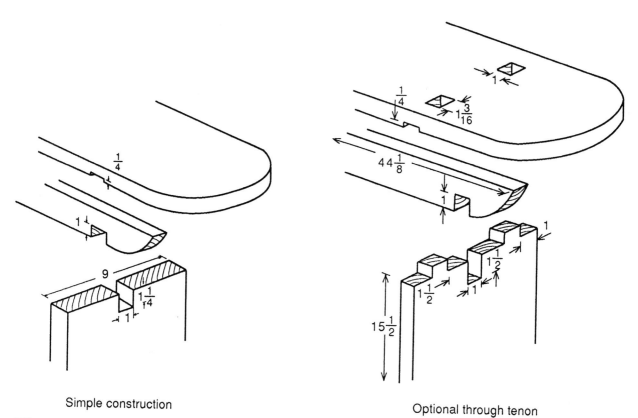

Simple construction

Optional through tenon

Illus. 6-8. *There are two options for joining the top to the ends. A simple approach employs a dado. A more sophisticated version uses a through tenon.*

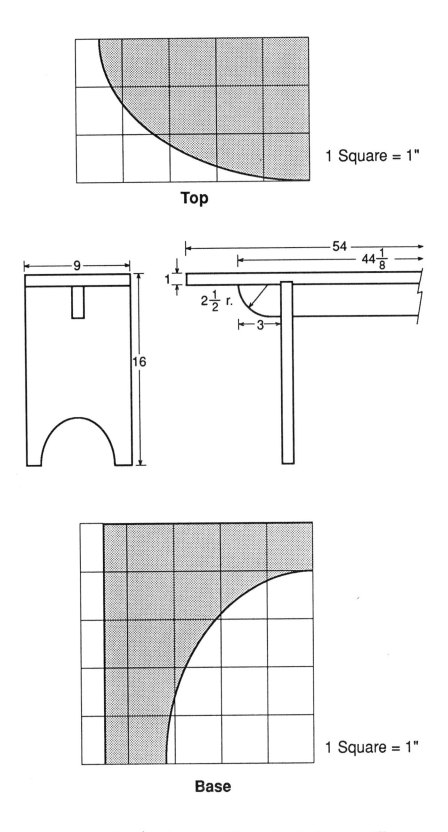

Illus. 6-9. *Plan for the South Union bench shown in Illus. 6-7.*

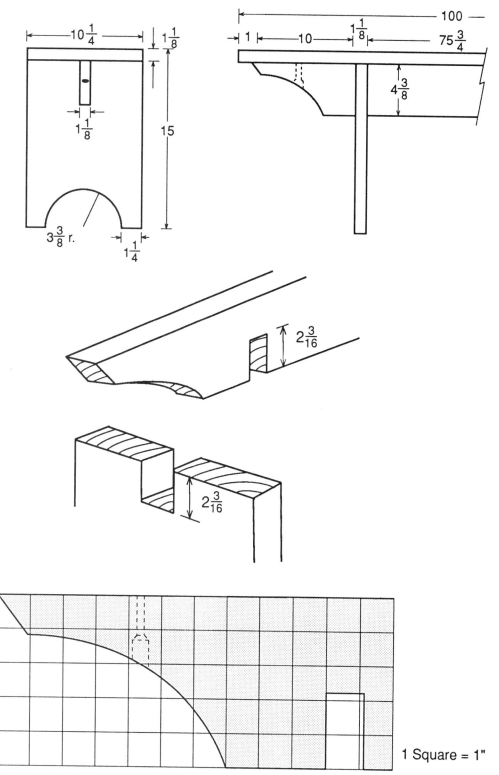

Illus. 6-10. *Plans for the Hancock Village bench shown in Illus. 6-11. Through tenons could also be used, as shown in Illus. 6-8.*

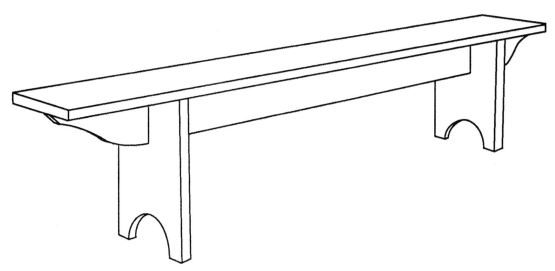

Illus. 6-11. *This is a meeting hall bench from Hancock Village. The stretchers, legs, and top are held together by five wood screws. The screws go through the stretcher into the top. This design allows the bench to be disassembled.*

CHAPTER 7

Step Stools

SHAKER ROOMS often had built-in closets that extended all the way to the ceiling. Objects that weren't frequently used were kept in the top compartments. Reaching these items required the use of a step stool. The ingenious Shakers developed a number of designs for step stools ranging from a simple design (shown in Illus. 7-1) to an elegant dovetail step stool (shown in Illus. 7-5). These designs can be used for a number of purposes. The three-step model shown in Illus. 7-6 makes an excellent plant stand.

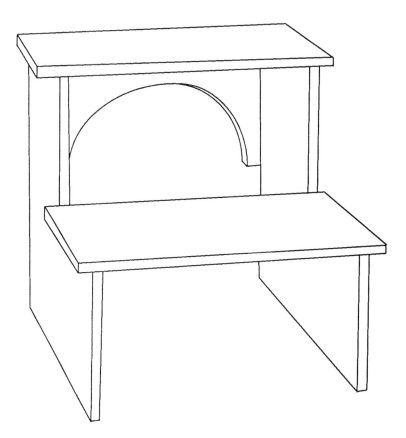

Illus. 7-1. *The Shakers made a large number of step stools. This walnut sewing step stool is very small. It's only 8 inches × 8½ inches and the design is rather delicate. It could be easily enlarged.*

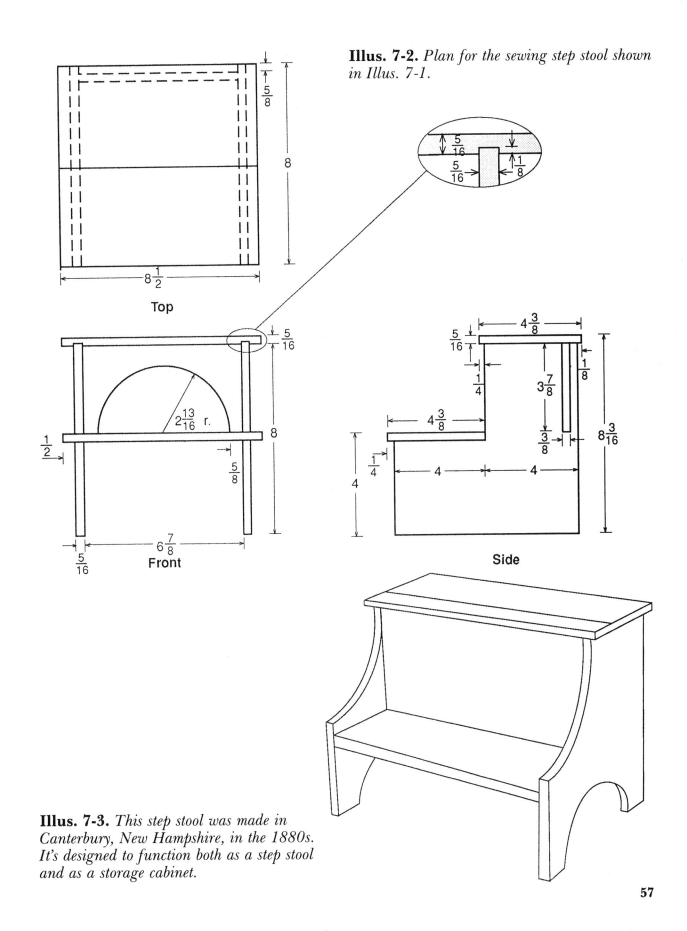

Illus. 7-2. *Plan for the sewing step stool shown in Illus. 7-1.*

Top

Front

Side

Illus. 7-3. *This step stool was made in Canterbury, New Hampshire, in the 1880s. It's designed to function both as a step stool and as a storage cabinet.*

57

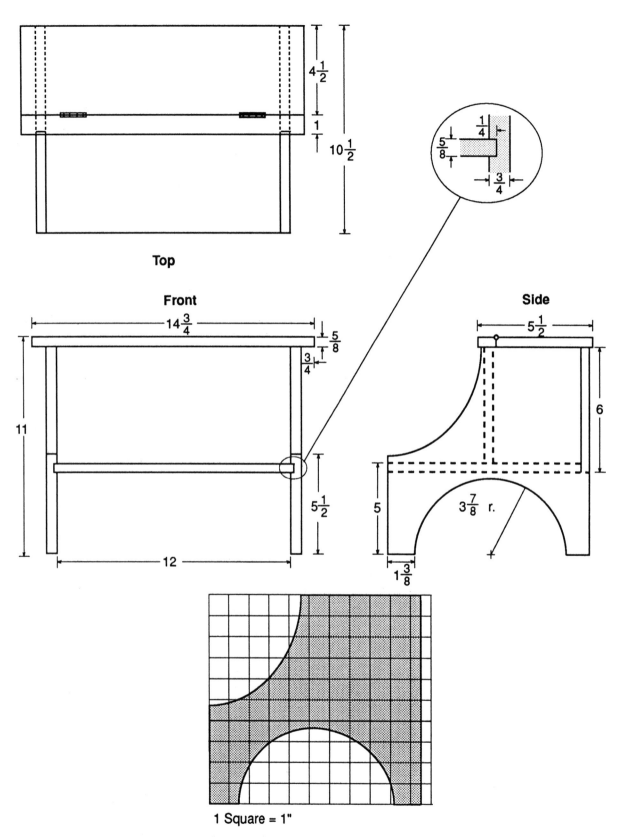

Top

Front

Side

$4\frac{1}{2}$

1

$10\frac{1}{2}$

$\frac{1}{4}$

$\frac{5}{8}$

$\frac{3}{4}$

$14\frac{3}{4}$

$\frac{5}{8}$

$\frac{3}{4}$

11

$5\frac{1}{2}$

12

$5\frac{1}{2}$

6

5

$3\frac{7}{8}$ r.

$1\frac{3}{8}$

1 Square = 1"

Illus. 7-4. *Detail of the Canterbury step stool shown in Illus. 7-3.*

Illus. 7-5 (right). *This example is typical of the Shakers' double step stool. The corners are dovetailed and two boards are used, so that the grain is continuous around the corners. The dovetail joinery should be done before the semi-circular corner is cut.*

Illus. 7-6 (left). *This three-step stool is from Hancock Village in Massachusetts. The original was made of painted pine, but just about any material could be used.*

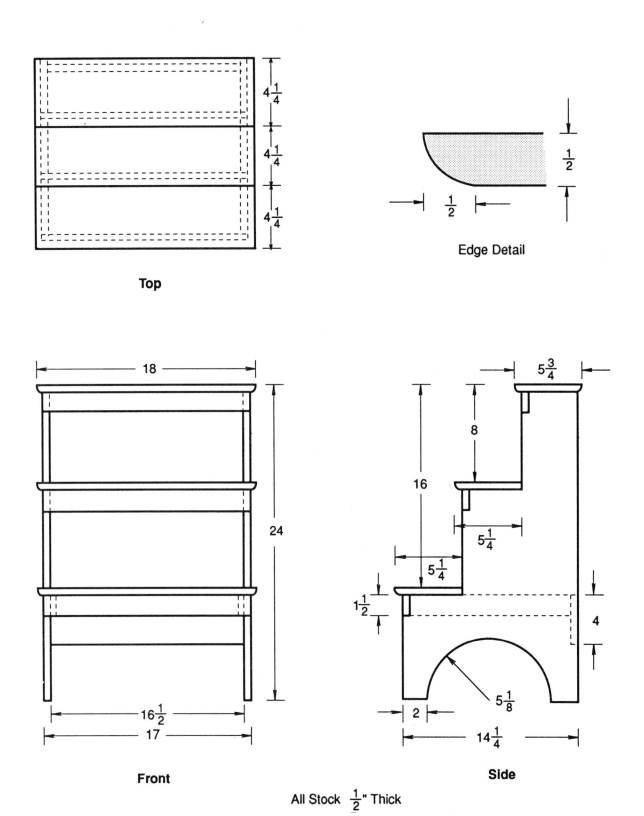

Top

Edge Detail

Front

Side

All Stock $\frac{1}{2}$" Thick

Illus. 7-7. *Plan for the three-step stool shown in Illus. 7-6.*

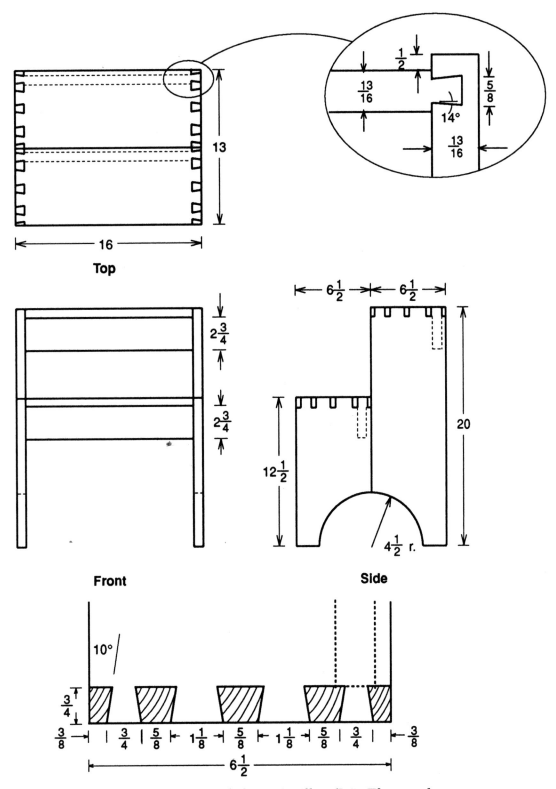

Illus. 7-8. *Plan for the step stool shown in Illus. 7-5. The stretcher which reinforces the step is towards the back of the step and is dovetailed into the side member.*

CHAPTER 8

Tables

THE SHAKERS MADE tables of many sizes and shapes. Illus. 8-10 shows a simple table with tapered legs. This table is small, but it can easily be made longer and taller. If you make it longer and taller, it would serve as an excellent dining table, especially if you add drop-leaf boards to the sides. The Shakers made some tables that had drop-leaf boards only on one side.

Also included in this chapter are designs for trestle tables the Shakers were fond of using. The most challenging table design, shown in Illus. 8-18–8-20, is a table with eight-sided tapered legs. This design originates from the Pleasant Hill, Kentucky, Shakers. A jig is used to support the leg while it is rough-cut on the band saw and then finished with a flush-trimming bit on the router table. The procedures for using the jig and the router table are shown in Illus. 8-21–8-29.

Illus. 8-33–8-47 feature plans and photographs of, and cutting techniques for, classic three-leg tables with turned columns.

Before taking on the table designs featured in this chapter, read the following sections on Using Taper Jigs and Cutting Mortise-and-Tenon Joints.

USING TAPER JIGS

Many of the Shaker tables have legs that are thinner on the bottom than on the top; these legs are called tapered legs.

Tapers are angled cuts made along the grain of the workpiece. When making tapered cuts on a long piece, use a jig. You can make your own or you can buy one. The shop-made taper *step jig* shown in Illus. 8-1 is used to make a taper on one side, opposite sides, or adjacent sides of a workpiece. A step jig, as the name implies, is a fixture using three notches or steps. The jig rides against the rip fence of the saw. The first cut is made with the workpiece resting on the middle or second step. To make a taper on the opposite side of the workpiece, use the third step on the jig. To make a taper on the adjacent side, rotate the workpiece 90 degrees.

The step jig is easy to make. Cut a piece of wood the width of the desired taper. Cut three pieces off the end and glue them, creating the step about ¼ inch high.

The *adjustable taper jig* has a hinge on one end and a locking mechanism on the opposite end. This jig can be adjusted to the desired angle. Illus. 8-2 shows a commercial version of the jig, but it is easy to make one out of scrap wood.

Illus. 8-1. *To make tapers on adjacent sides using the taper jig, use the second step for both cuts. After the first cut, rotate the piece 90 degrees for the second cut.*

Illus. 8-2. *This commercially available jig is adjustable. It has a taper of one inch per foot.*

CUTTING MORTISE-AND-TENON JOINTS

The mortise-and-tenon joint is one of the strongest joints. It is used for frame work in projects such as chairs and tables. Illus. 8-3 shows the process involved in cutting a tenon on the band saw.

With the advent of powerful plunge routers, it is now easier to make the mor-

Illus. 8-3. *The tenon requires two series of cuts. Cut the shoulder first with a crosscut, as shown on the bottom piece. Make the neck with a rip cut. Here the progression of these cuts is shown.*

Illus. 8-4. *The corners on this tenon are bevelled. The bevelled corners fit the round mortise made by a router bit. The flat surfaces allow for a glue release that is similar to that on the flutes of a dowel.*

tise. The mortise made with a router requires a tenon that will fit the round corner left by the router bit. The solution is to design a tenon that will fit the round mortise.

One solution is to make the tenon corners angled (Illus. 8-4). This solves the problem of fitting a square tenon into a round corner. It also solves the problem of releasing glue pressure. The 45-degree corner will snugly fit the round corner, but it will also allow for the escape of captured glue. This is the idea behind the fluted dowel.

The tenon requires two types of cuts. A crosscut is used to define the shoulder of the tenon. This can be done on the band saw, but is often done on the table saw. It is often better to crosscut with the table saw so that the crosscut is slightly (1/32 inch) deeper than the rip cut used to define the tenon. This ensures that the corner cut will

be complete, and provides a place for the excess glue.

After the crosscut is made, a rip cut is used to define the tenon. The band saw excels at this type of cutting because of its ability to cut into a corner. Another advantage is that the workpiece lies flat on the table for this process rather than having an end straight up in the air, as is the case when the table saw is used.

Cut the mortise first and then cut the tenon to fit into it. The setup for doing the rip cut on the tenon is the usual setup for ripping, except that a stop block is used to stop the cut. Using a micro-adjusting jig facilitates the final cutting of the joint. A micro-adjuster is an accessory that fits into the rip fence. It moves the fence by rotating a thread.

Cut the edge of the tenon first (Illus. 8-5). This is the least critical of the cuts, especially if the mortise is round. If the mortise is round, do the final fitting with the 45-degree bevel cut. Next, make the other shoulder cut (Illus. 8-6 and 8-7).

Make the cuts slightly oversized, and use the micro-adjuster for the final fit.

If you have a round mortise, bevel the corners of the tenon. Tilt the table to 45 degrees (Illus. 8-8). Make the bevel cuts by cutting the opposite corners with the same fence setting (Illus. 8-9).

Illus. 8-5. *It is better if you make the edge initial test cut first.*

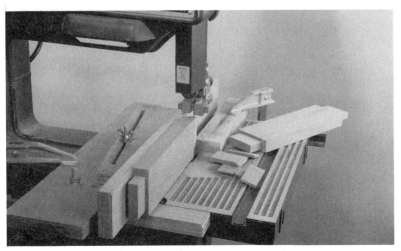

Illus. 8-6. *Make the fit slightly oversized and then slowly take off material until it fits.*

Illus. 8-7. *Shown here is the position of the stop block. The blade should be on the outside of the tenon so that the waste falls away from the fence rather than between the fence and the blade.*

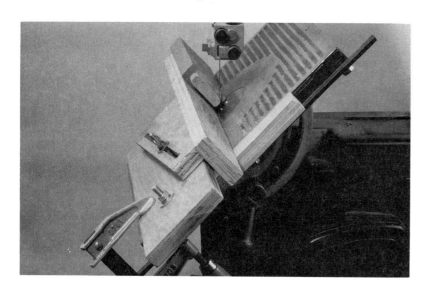

Illus. 8-8. *Bevel the corners of the tenon by tilting the table to 45 degrees.*

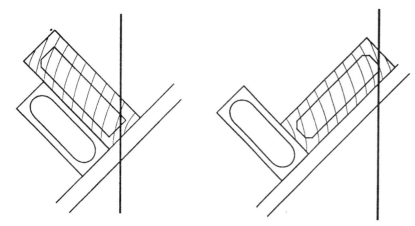

Illus. 8-9. *Make the bevel cuts by cutting the opposite corners with the same fence setting.*

Illus. 8-10. *The Shakers made a number of tables with tapered legs. This small table is appropriate to be used as a side table or a lamp table. The same design could be enlarged for a dining-room table; a drop-leaf could also be added. The stretcher is mortised into the legs. This example is typical of Shaker tables in which different types of woods were used. The legs are hard maple, and the top is butternut.*

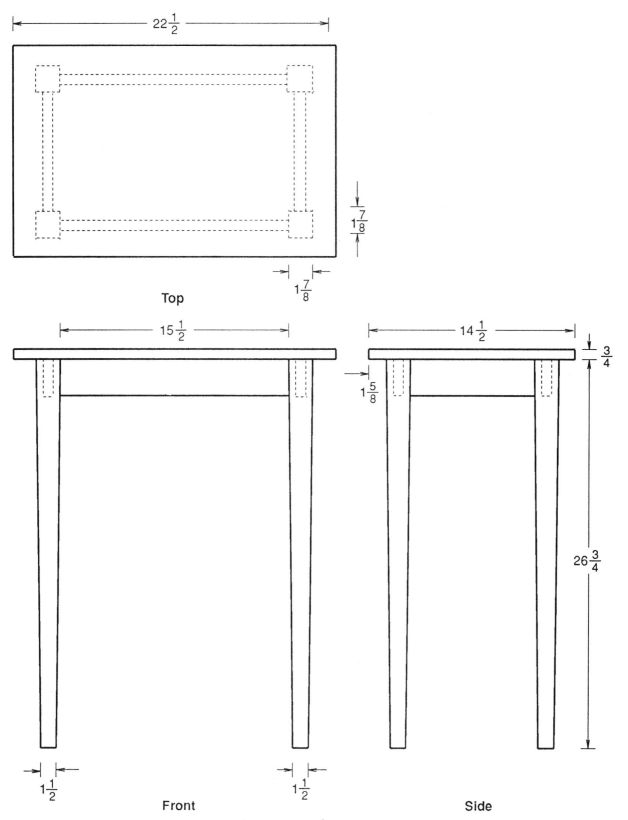

Illus. 8-11. *Plan for the tapered-leg table shown in Illus. 8-10.*

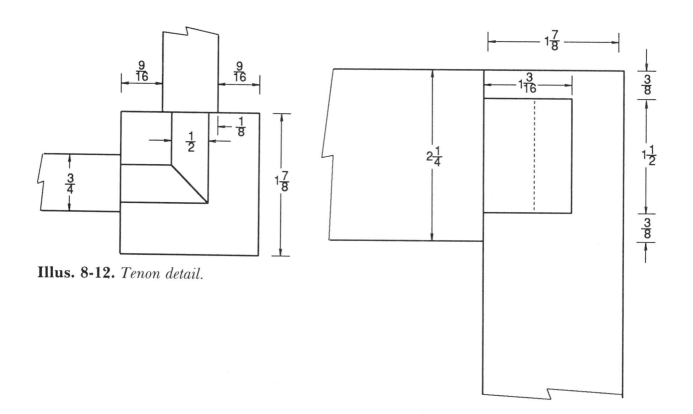

Illus. 8-12. *Tenon detail.*

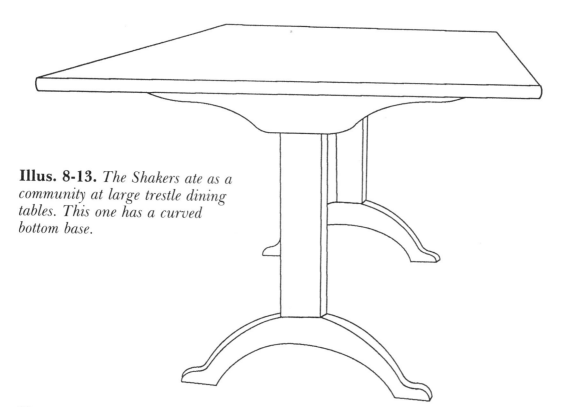

Illus. 8-13. *The Shakers ate as a community at large trestle dining tables. This one has a curved bottom base.*

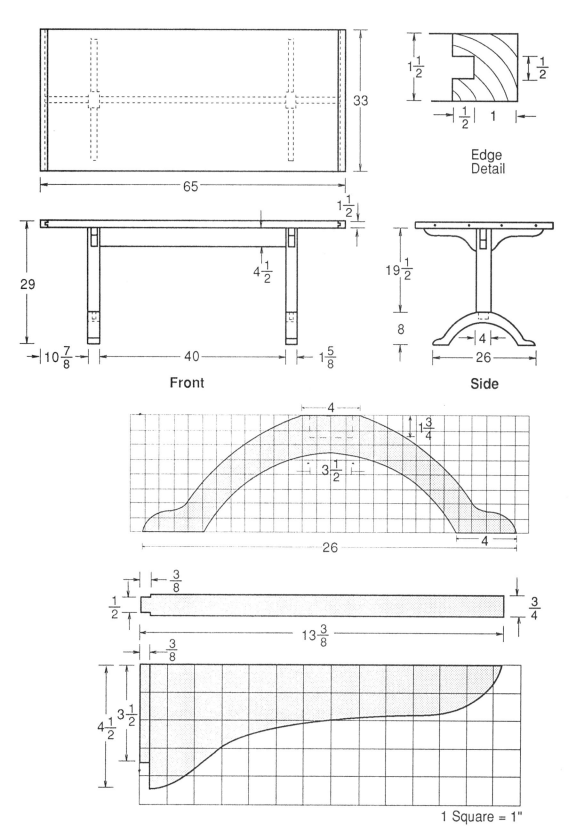

Illus. 8-14. *Plan for the trestle table shown in Illus. 8-13.*

Illus. 8-15. *This delicate side table is a unique Shaker table, because it appears to be more decorative than useful. The bottom base has a gentle curve.*

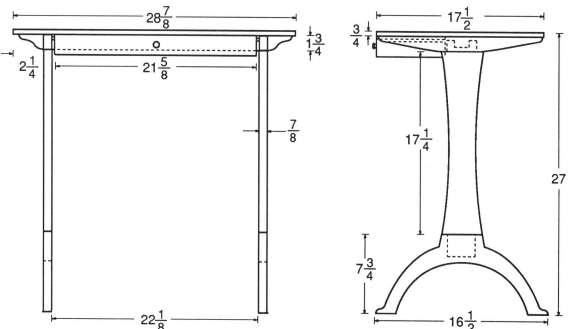

Illus. 8-16. *Front and side detail for the side table shown in Illus. 8-15.*

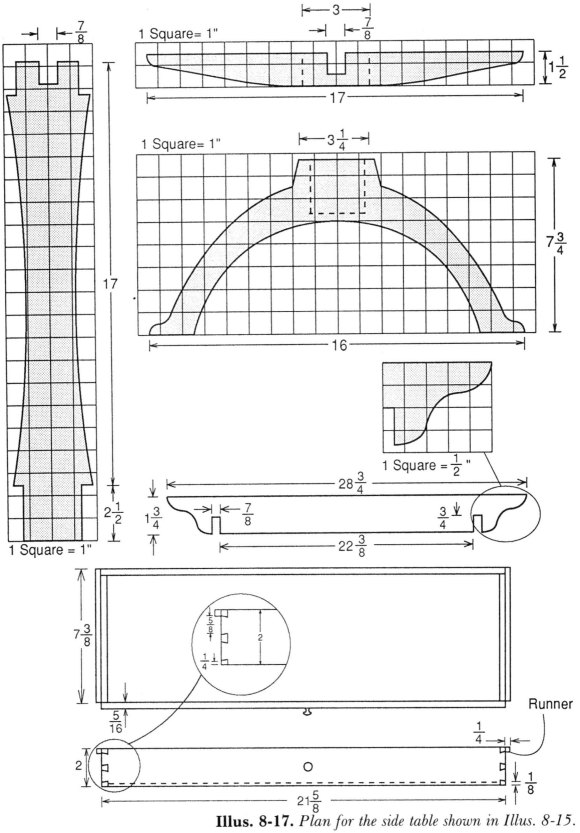

Illus. 8-17. *Plan for the side table shown in Illus. 8-15.*

Illus. 8-18. *This table was made at Pleasant Hill, Kentucky, and is unique because of the eight-sided tapered legs. The taper angles to a small footprint. The stretchers are mortised into the legs. These legs would be very time-consuming to make by hand. With a band-saw jig and a router table, a very accurate leg is easily produced. Illus. 8-21–8-29 show how to cut the tapered legs.*

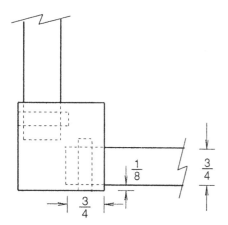

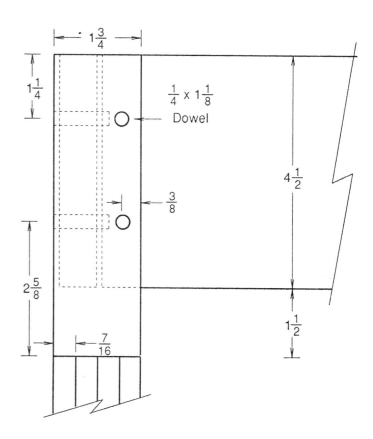

Illus. 8-19. *Mortise-and-tenon detail for the tapered-leg table shown in Illus. 8-18.*

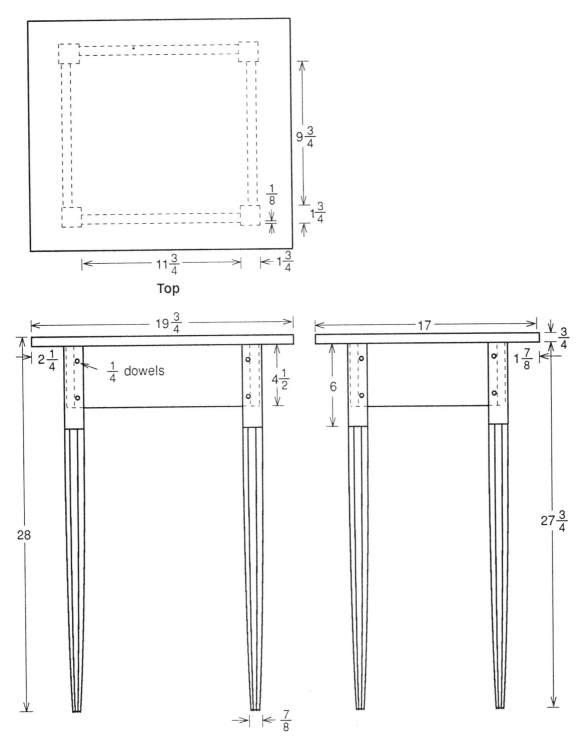

Top

Illus. 8-20. *Detail for the tapered-leg table shown in Illus. 8-18.*

73

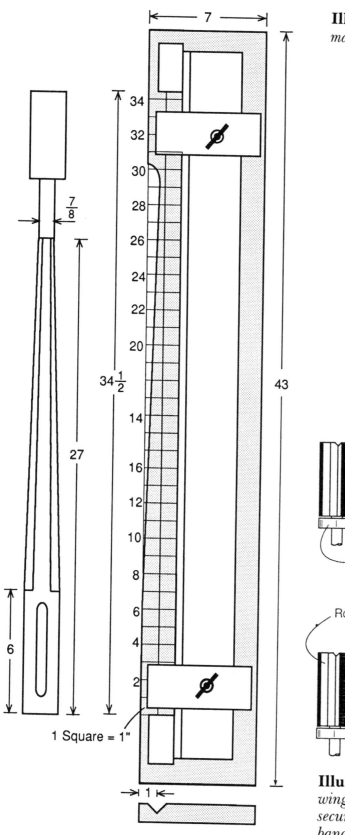

Illus. 8-21. *The design of the jig used to make the eight-sided tapered legs.*

7

34
32
30
28
26
24
22
20

$34\frac{1}{2}$

43

14

16

12

10

8

6

4

2

$\frac{7}{8}$

27

6

1 Square = 1"

1

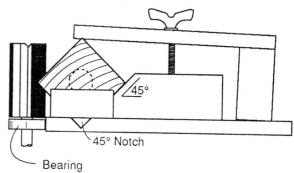

45°

45° Notch

Bearing

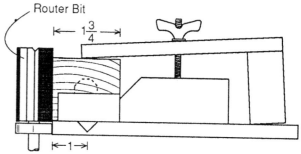

Router Bit

$1\frac{3}{4}$

1

Illus. 8-22. *The jig secures the leg with two wing nuts. A notch in the base of the jig secures the wood at a 45-degree angle to the band saw and the router table.*

Illus. 8-23. *The leg is held in a V-block for the first corner cut on the table saw.*

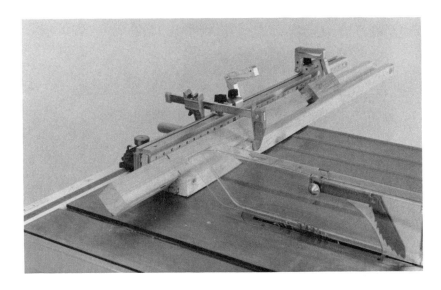

Illus. 8-24. *A large dado is cut at the bottom of the leg. Two series of crosscuts are made around the leg, and the material between the two cuts is cut away on the band saw using a fence.*

Illus. 8-25. *A rub block is used in contact with the jig to make the first band-saw cuts.*

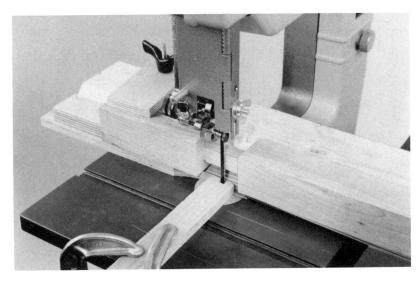

Illus. 8-26. *Keep the jig in contact with the rub block during the band-saw cut.*

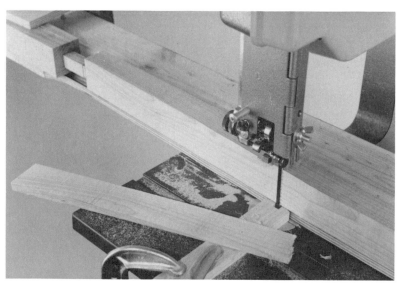

Illus. 8-27. *The completed cut.*

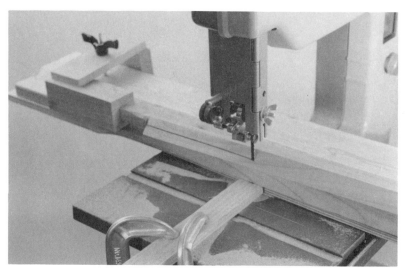

Illus. 8-28. *Rotate the workpiece and make another cut.*

Illus. 8-29. *After the initial material is wasted on the band saw, the jig is used on the router table with a bottom-bearing flush-trimming bit. Rotate the workpiece after each cut, to finish all eight sides.*

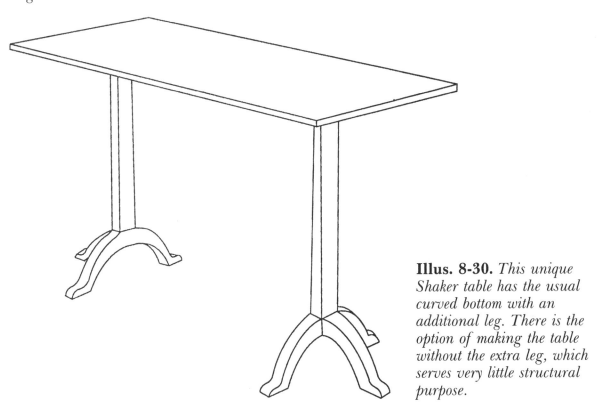

Illus. 8-30. *This unique Shaker table has the usual curved bottom with an additional leg. There is the option of making the table without the extra leg, which serves very little structural purpose.*

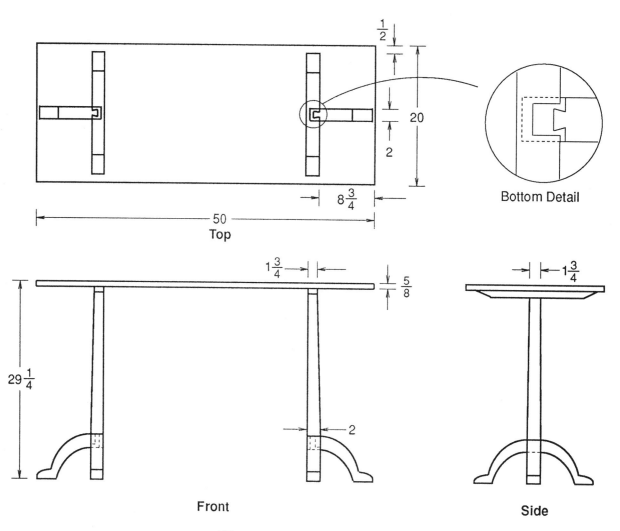

Illus. 8-31. *Plan for the Shaker table shown in Illus. 8-30.*

Illus. 8-32. *Curved leg detail for the Shaker table shown in Illus. 8-30.*

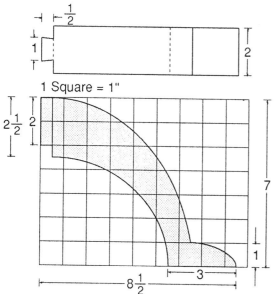

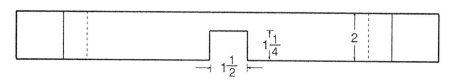

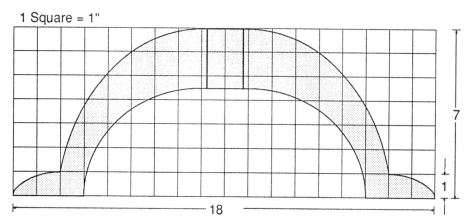

1 Square = 1"

Continuation of curved leg detail.

Illus. 8-33. *This three-legged round table is typical of many similar tables designed by the Shakers. This table is the simplest to make and doesn't require the turning skill of some of the more complex tables. The top is cut with a band saw and a circle-cutting jig or a router. The post is turned, and the three legs are dovetailed into the post.*

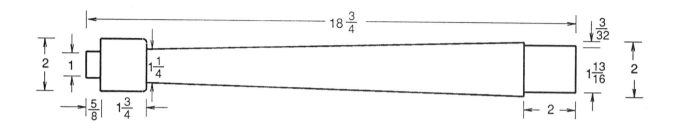

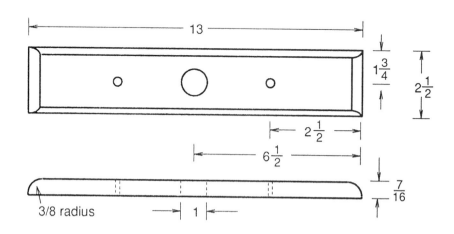

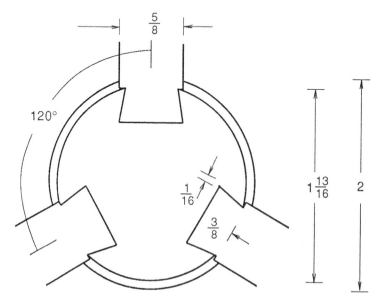

Illus. 8-34. *Leg detail for the three-legged round table shown in Illus. 8-33.*

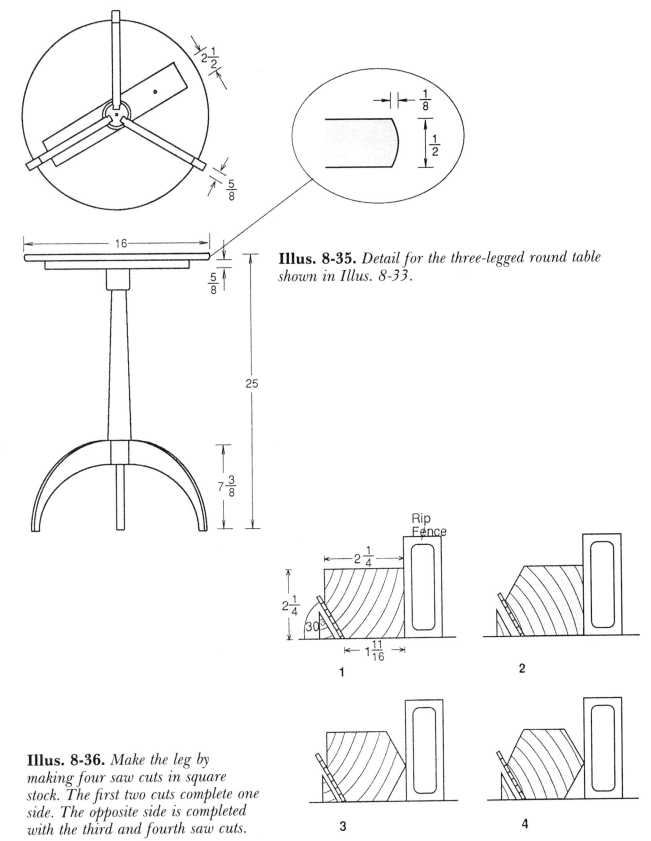

Illus. 8-35. *Detail for the three-legged round table shown in Illus. 8-33.*

Illus. 8-36. *Make the leg by making four saw cuts in square stock. The first two cuts complete one side. The opposite side is completed with the third and fourth saw cuts.*

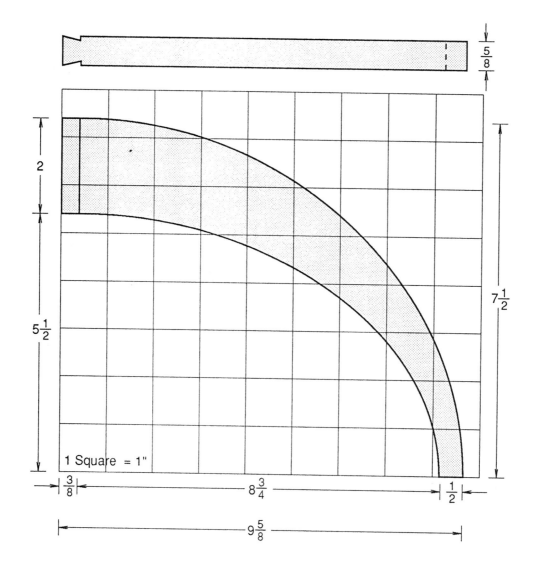

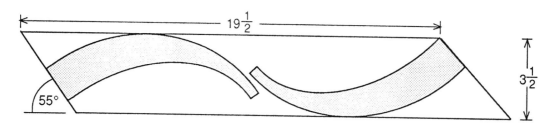

Illus. 8-37. *Leg-pattern detail for the three-legged round table shown in Illus. 8-33.*

Illus. 8-38. *After the leg is turned, make the dovetail on the router table with the leg's flat side lying flat on the table. You may need to extend the fence on your router table to keep the work straight, as shown here. Use a flip stop to limit the depth of the cut.*

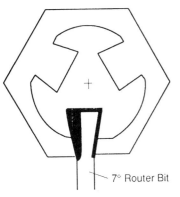

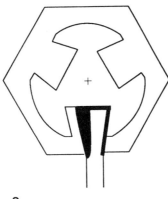

7° Router Bit

1

2

Illus. 8-39. *Use a seven-degree dovetail router bit and make two passes, one from each direction, to guarantee that the dovetail slot is centered.*

Illus. 8-40. *A close-up of the dovetail bit.*

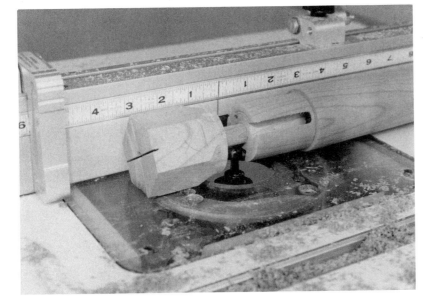

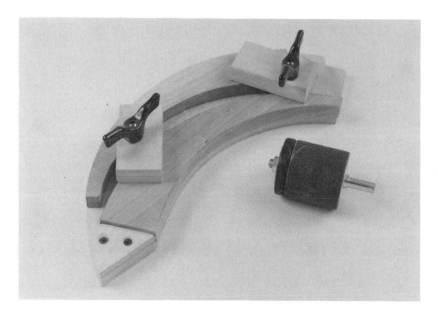

Illus. 8-41. *This jig is designed to hold two legs so that the inside and the outside of the legs can both be sanded at the same time. The sander has a solid phenolic disc at its bottom which does not rotate and functions like a flush-trimming bit. It is handy for situations like this, when the grain is not straight.*

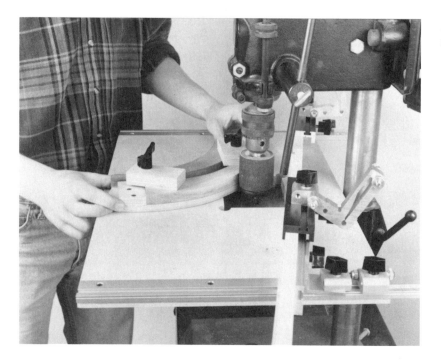

Illus. 8-42. *Use the sander in a drill press.*

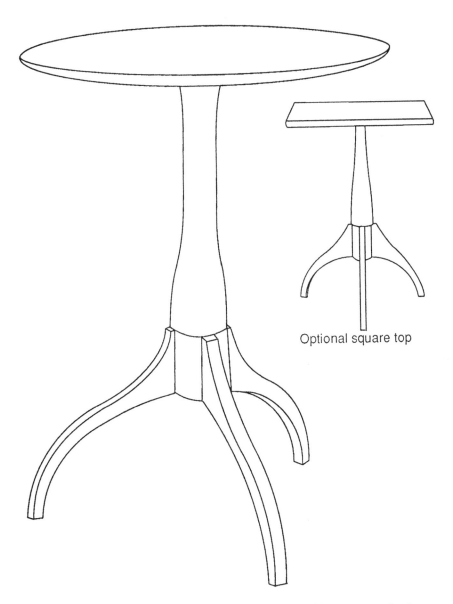

Optional square top

Illus. 8-43. *The flowing curves of this table are a typical Shaker design element. An optional square top is used on some of these tables. A drawer may be added to the bottom of the square top.*

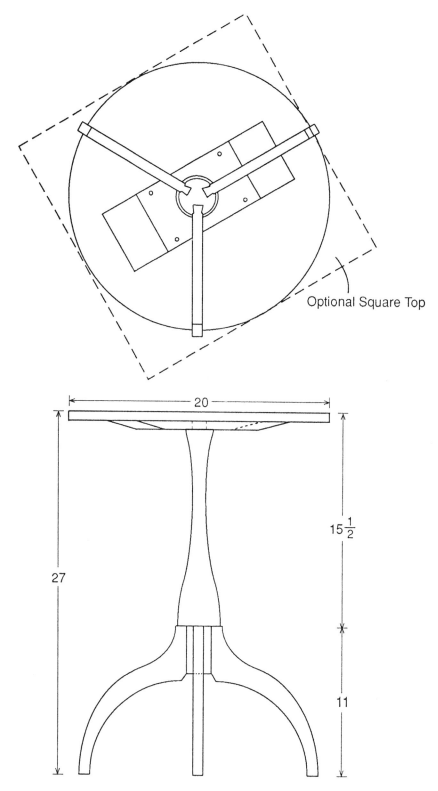

Optional Square Top

Illus. 8-44. *Side and top detail for the Shaker table shown in Illus. 8-43.*

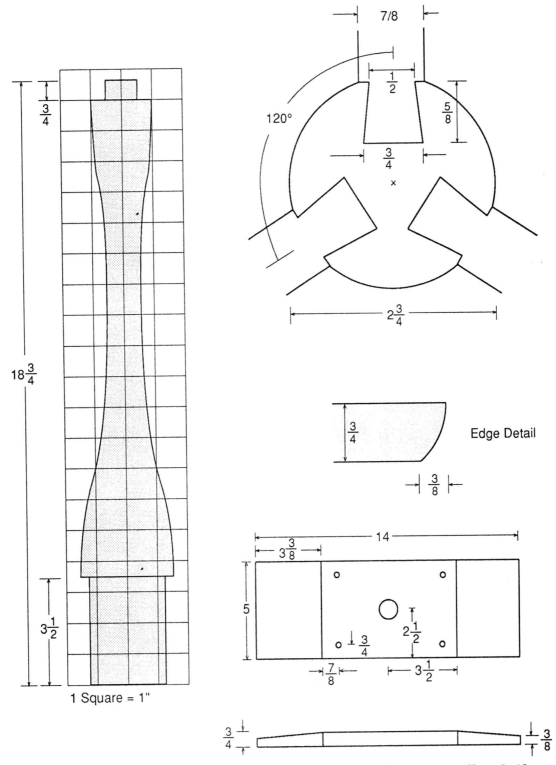

Illus. 8-45. *Leg and dovetail detail for the Shaker table shown in Illus. 8-43.*

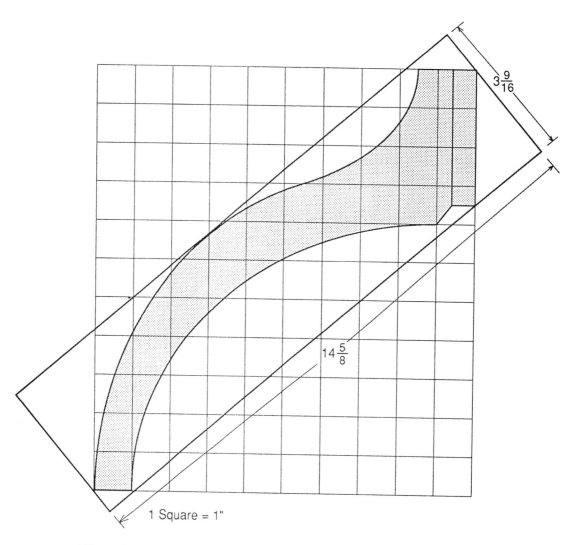

Illus. 8-46. *Leg detail for the Shaker table shown in Illus. 8-43.*

CHAPTER 9

Chairs

THE SHAKERS STARTED to make chairs for their own use, and got so efficient at making them that they soon became one of the items that were sold to the outside world. As the industry grew, the Shakers expanded the variety of styles and sizes and published a catalogue. The chair shown in Illus. 9-1 is a simple model that is a good design for those making their first attempt at chair making. If you do not have a lathe, the legs can be made from dowels 1⅜ inches in diameter. These dowels are often available from lumberyards. The curved seat slats are made on the band saw.

Most woodworkers agree that the most difficult piece of furniture to make is a chair. I often make tables featuring Shaker designs; however, making chairs to complement these tables has always been troublesome because I'm not an efficient turner. To make Shaker chairs quickly requires hours of practice at the lathe.

The Shakers made one chair that did not have turned legs. It was made in Hancock Village, Massachusetts, and was called the Weaver's Chair. It is shown in Illus. 9-8. The Weaver's Chair was taller than average and was used at a loom or countertop. Its legs are straight, and there is one single slat for the back. This chair is

Illus. 9-1. *This two-slat dining chair is typical of the Shaker chairs, even though it does not have the turned details of the Shaker rockers or the more elaborate dining chairs. The legs can be turned or can be made from maple dowels 1⅜" in diameter. Illus. 9-2–9-7 show details and cutting techniques for making this chair.*

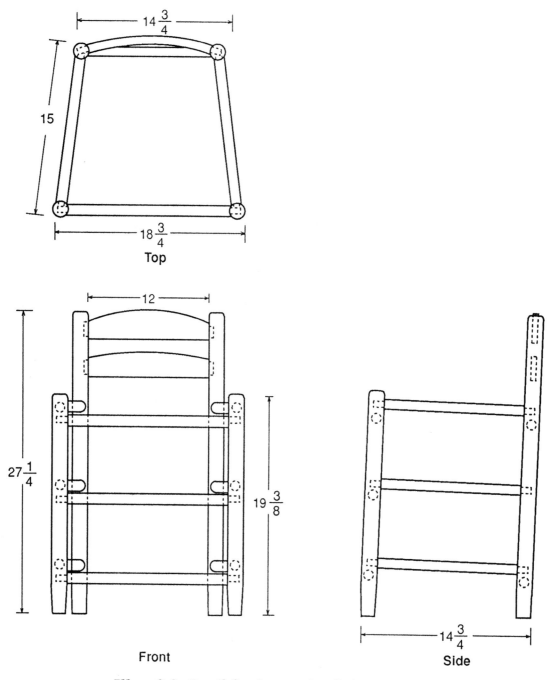

Illus. 9-2. *Detail for the two-slat dining chair shown in Illus. 9-1.*

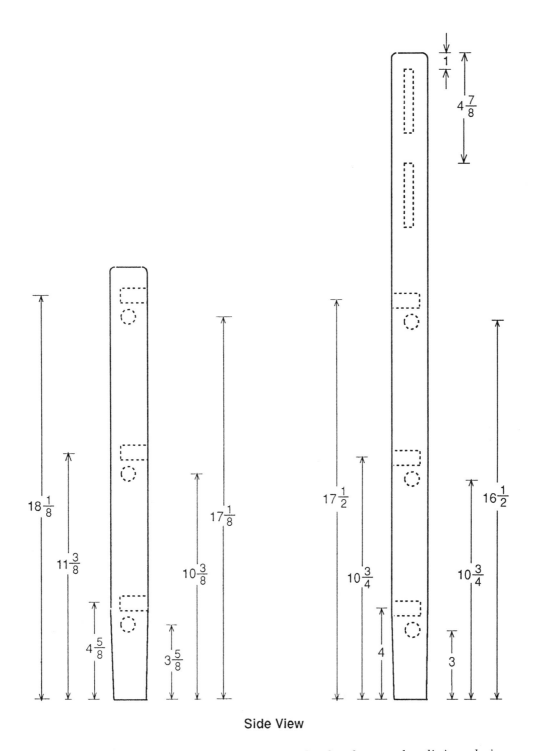

Side View

Illus. 9-3. *Detail of leg and stretcher holes for the two-slat dining chair shown in Illus. 9-1.*

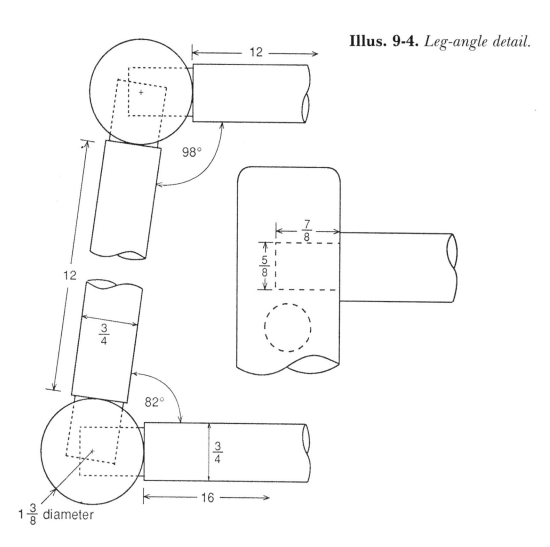

Illus. 9-4. *Leg-angle detail.*

12

98°

12

$\frac{3}{4}$

82°

$1\frac{3}{8}$ diameter

$\frac{3}{4}$

16

$\frac{7}{8}$

$\frac{5}{8}$

Illus. 9-5. *Detail of top slat.*

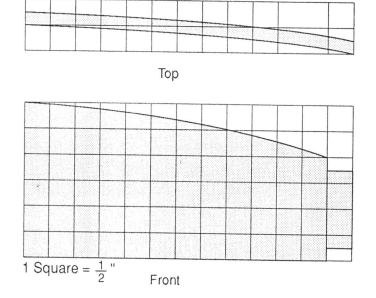

Top

1 Square = $\frac{1}{2}$"

Front

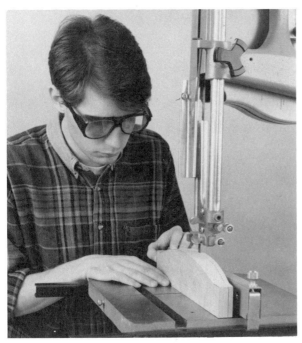

Illus. 9-6. *The curve of the slat is made with the convex side against the fence.*

Illus. 9-7. *Finish the concave side with a sanding drum on a drill press. A micro-adjuster on this drill press allows multiple passes to be adjusted in small increments.*

Illus. 9-8. *The chair on the left is The Weaver's Chair from Hancock Village in Massachusetts, which was made by Seth Reed. The chair on the right is an adaptation. The Weaver's Chair is the only type of chair made by the Shakers that was not turned. It was taller than average and was used at a loom or a countertop. The legs were straight, and there was one single slat. It is easy to make because the holes for the front and back are drilled at 90 degrees. The stretchers between the front and the back of the chair are angled at five degrees. By using jigs, you can easily make the chair to a high degree of accuracy.*

Illus. 9-9. *Note the curved leg on this chair, which is an adaptation of The Weaver's Chair.*

easy to make because the holes for the front and back legs are drilled at 90 degrees. The stretchers between the front and back legs are angled at 5 degrees. By using jigs and fixtures and the router table, which are illustrated in this chapter, you can easily make a variation of the Weaver's Chair to a high degree of accuracy.

Because of the manufacturing techniques, this chair avoids the complexity of most seating projects. Illus. 9-10–9-12 show the chair details. There are two slats. The stretchers angle rearwards slightly because the back legs are slightly shorter than the front legs. The hole for the top stretcher for the front leg is 17¼ inches

Illus. 9-10 (right). *Detail for the chairs shown in Illus. 9-8 and 9-9.*

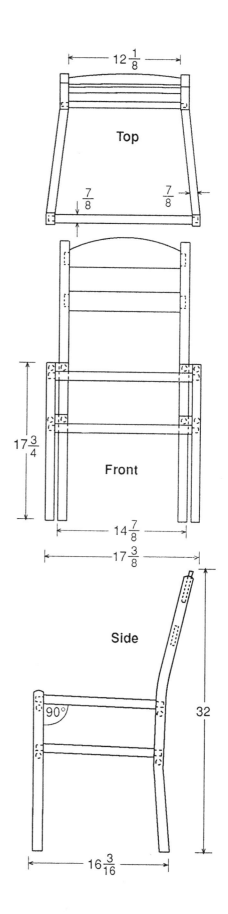

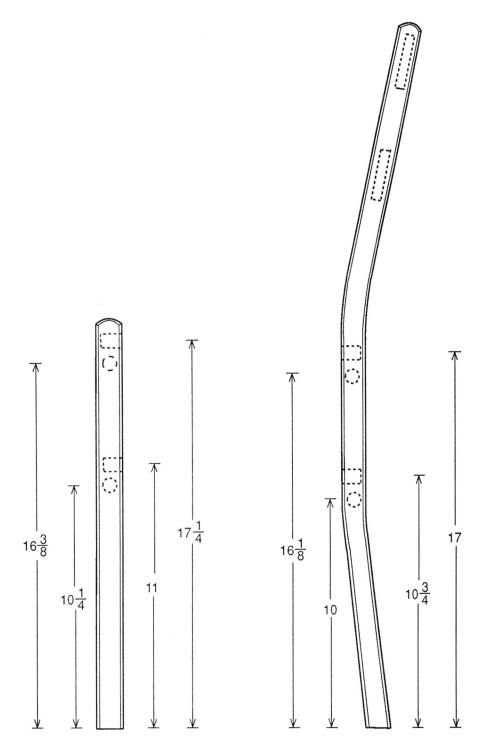

Illus. 9-11. *Leg and hole detail.*

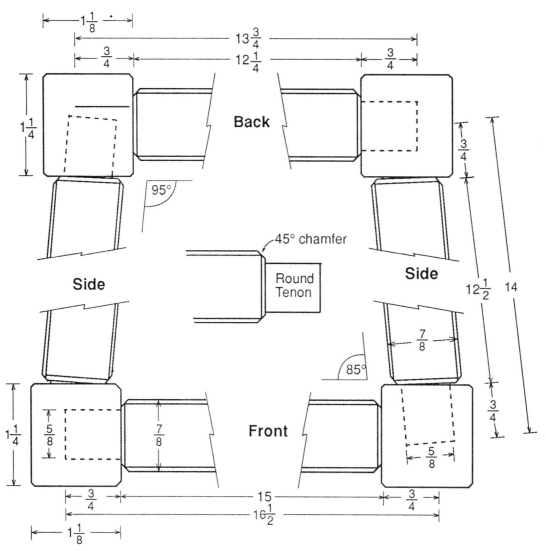

Illus. 9-12. *Detail for a round tenon and holes.*

from the floor, whereas the corresponding hole in the back leg is 17 inches from the floor, so the stretcher angles from the front leg to the back leg downwards ¼ inch. The legs are rough-cut on the band saw and finished to their final dimensions with a fixture which is made to hold the leg in relationship to the flush-trimming bit. This fixture is depicted in Illus. 9-14–9-16. A slight 45-degree bevel is put on the corners of the legs and the stretcher with a 45-degree router bit with a bearing. This is shown in Illus. 9-17.

A large dowel cutter, shown in Illus.

9-18, is used in the drill press to cut the round tenon on the end of the stretcher. The holes are drilled in the back legs at a 5-degree angle with a platform, shown in Illus. 9-19 and 9-20. The back slats are made with a series of cuts. The first cross-cuts are made on the table saw; these cuts trim the shoulders of the tenons. The tenons are then rough-cut on the band saw, as shown in Illus. 9-23, and then trimmed on the router table with a 1-inch-diameter router bit, as shown in Illus. 9-24. After being rough-cut on the band saw, the chair slat is attached to a half-pattern jig and is trimmed to the finished dimension with a flush-trimming router bit, as shown in Illus. 9-25.

To make the curve in the back slat, a "curve block" (Illus. 9-26) is used; this is a piece of wood the length of the chair slat

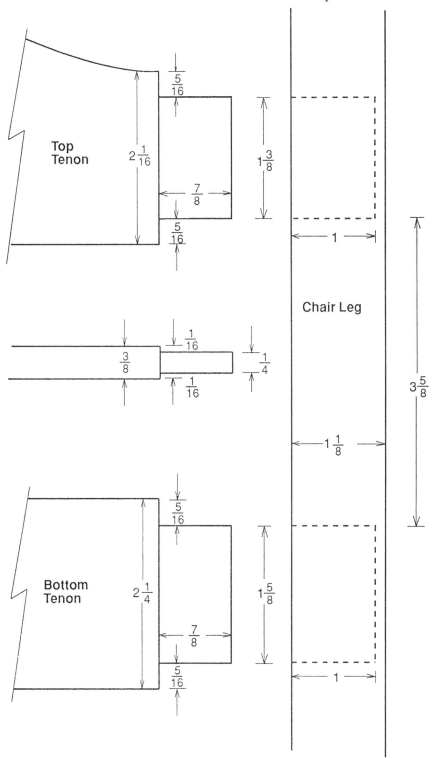

Illus. 9-13. *The top and bottom tenons detail.*

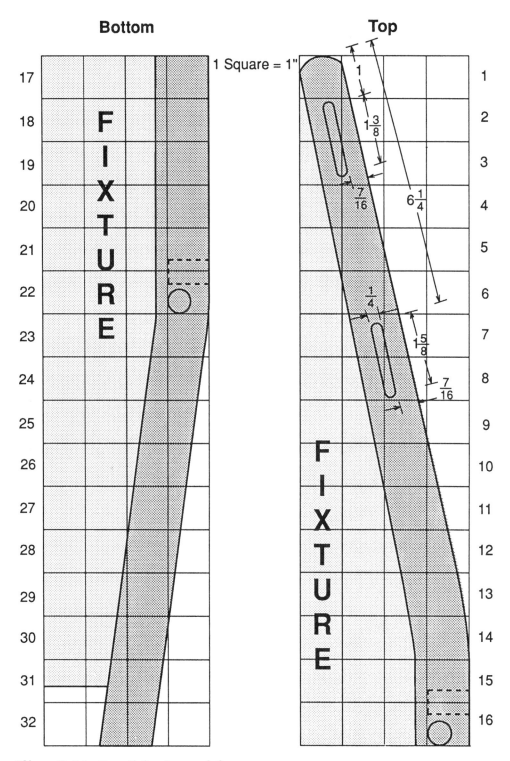

Bottom **Top**

1 Square = 1"

Illus. 9-14. *Detail for leg and fixture.*

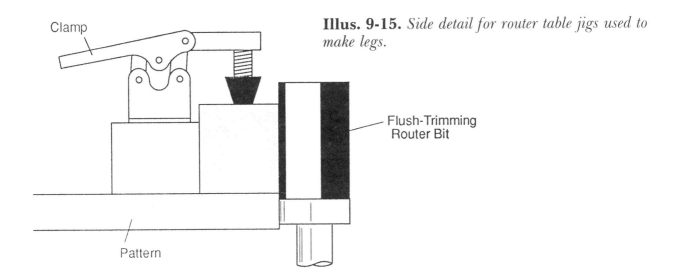

Clamp

Illus. 9-15. *Side detail for router table jigs used to make legs.*

Flush-Trimming
Router Bit

Pattern

Illus. 9-16. *This jig is used to cut the back of the chair leg.*

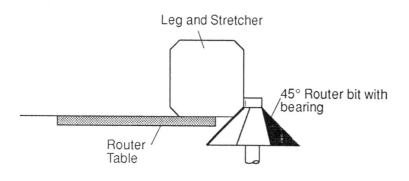

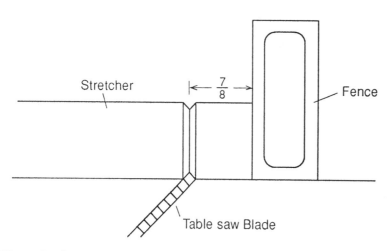

Illus. 9-17. *The corner of the leg and stretcher is trimmed with a 45-degree bit on the router table. The end of the stretcher is cut on a table saw with the blade tilted at 45 degrees.*

Illus. 9-18. *A large dowel cutter is used in the drill press to cut the round tenon on the end of the stretcher.*

Illus. 9-19. *A platform which angles the workpiece at five degrees is used to drill the angled holes for the stretchers between the front and the back of the chair. The workpiece rests on a fixture, which is a piece of 2 × 4 cut to match the back of the chair.*

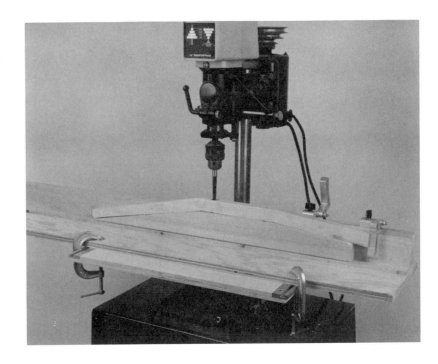

Illus. 9-20. *End view of drilling fixture and platform.*

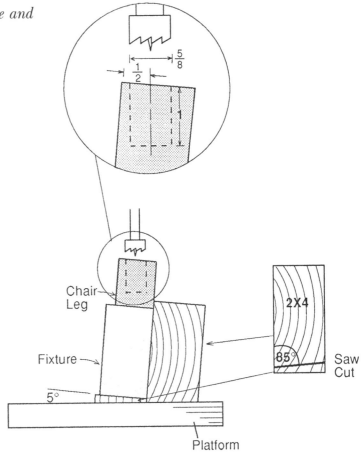

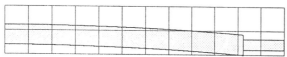

Top View of Back Slats

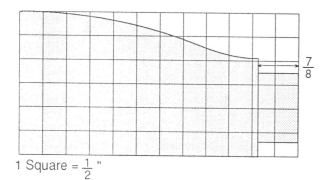

$\frac{7}{8}$

1 Square = $\frac{1}{2}$ "

Front View of Back Slats

$\frac{7}{8}$

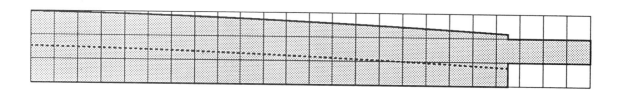

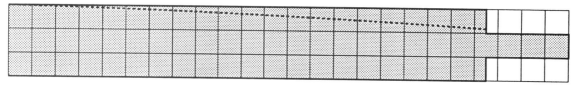

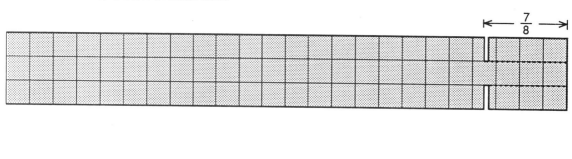

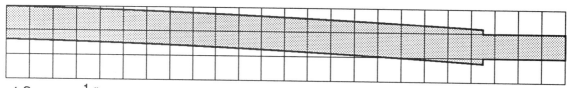

1 Square = $\frac{1}{4}$ "

Illus. 9-22. *Top detail for back slat.*

Illus. 9-23. *The tenon on the back slat is made by making a crosscut on the table saw and then cutting the cheek waste on the band saw.*

Illus. 9-24. *The final tenon sizing is done on the router table with a one-inch bit.*

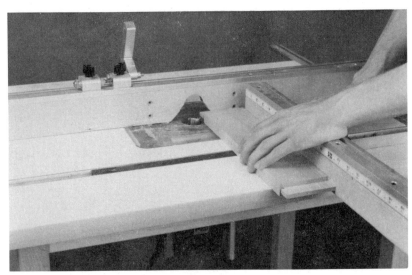

Illus. 9-25. *This jig is designed to cut half of the curve on the top slat. After one-half of the piece is completed, it is then rotated to complete the second half. This jig should be used with a starting pin.*

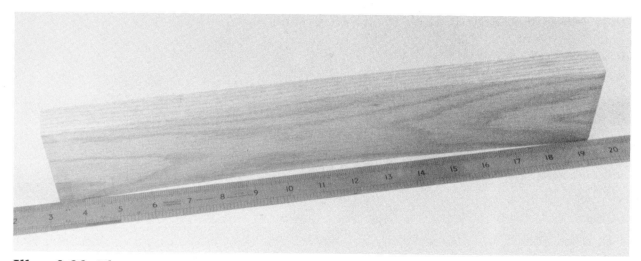

Illus. 9-26. *The curve on the slats is made with the use of a "curve block." A piece of wood the size of the chair slat is arched so that ³⁄₁₆" of the material is removed.*

that has a concave piece of material cut out that measures about ³⁄₁₆ inch. The curved block is attached to the chair slat with double-faced masking tape, and a two-inch rub block is also attached to the rip fence with double-faced tape. The chair slat is fed into the blade, and a tapered piece of waste is removed (Illus. 9-27). The curved block is rotated and turned end-for-end, and the end on the opposite piece of the chair slat is trimmed off (Illus. 9-28). The curved block and the workpiece are passed through a disc or a belt sander, and the roughness left by the band saw is removed as shown in Illus. 9-29. The concave side of the chair is then finished. If you have an inflatable drum on a drum sander, this is probably one of the best ways to finish it (Illus. 9-30). The convex side is then placed against the band-saw fence, and the opposite side is cut, as shown in Illus. 9-31 and 9-32.

Illus. 9-27. *The chair slat is attached to the straight side of the curve block with double-faced tape. A two-inch block is attached to the rip fence with double-faced tape. The middle of the rip-fence block should be aligned with the saw blade. The workpiece is fed into the blade, and a tapered waste piece is removed.*

Illus. 9-28. *Rotate the curve block and the workpiece end for end and make the same cut on the opposite end.*

Illus. 9-29. *The curve block and the workpiece are then passed through a disc sander. The retaining board is clamped to the table. After each pass, the retaining board can be advanced forward slightly.*

Illus. 9-30. *The final sanding can be done on an inflatable drum, as shown here, or by hand.*

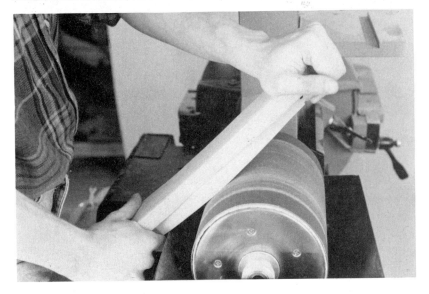

Illus. 9-31. *This photo shows that the waste is thicker in the middle and thinner on the outside. The inside can be sanded with a sanding drum on the drill press, as shown in Illus. 9-7.*

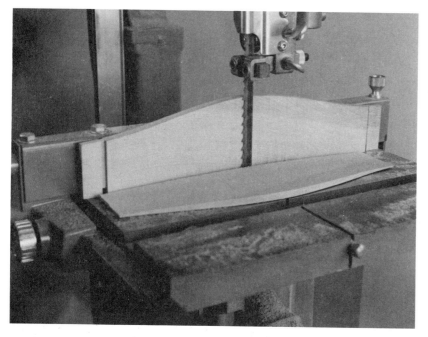

Illus. 9-32. *Place the waste under the slat to keep it flat on the table when crosscutting the final cut for the tenon.*

CHAPTER 10

Steam-Bending Projects

OVAL BOXES

The oval box is one of the most popular items the Shakers made. It is highly valued for its simple beauty (Illus. 10-1). The oval boxes represented a relatively small part of the total number of goods produced by the Shaker communities. They were produced consistently from the late 18th century to the middle of this century. The Shakers originally made these boxes for their own use, but found a ready market outside of their communities.

During the century and a half that the Shakers made boxes, their construction methods changed very little. Most of the original boxes were made with hard maple or birch sides (or bands) and pine tops and bottoms (Illus. 10-2). Both hard maple and birch can be used in thin dimensions and the box will still be strong. However, these woods respond to changes in seasonal humidity, making them a poor choice for the tops and bottoms because of

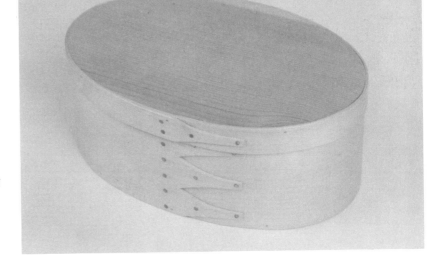

Illus. 10-1. *A traditional Shaker box. The side or bands are made of hard maple and are secured with copper tacks. The top and bottom are made of quartersawed white pine.*

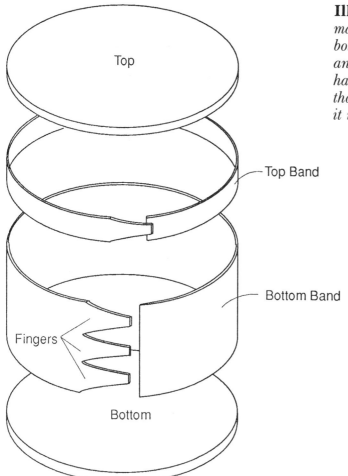

Illus. 10-2. *The traditional Shaker box is made out of four pieces of wood. The top and bottom are usually made of pine between 3/16 and 1/4 inch thick and the bands are made of hardwood. The traditional shape is oval. Even though there is not much material in this box, it is surprisingly strong.*

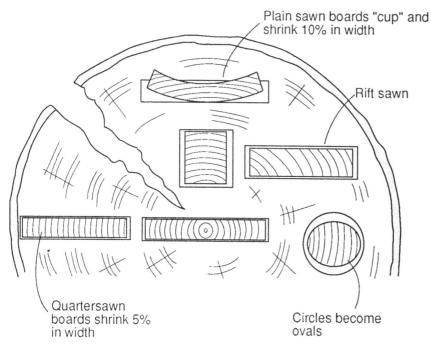

Plain sawn boards "cup" and shrink 10% in width

Rift sawn

Quartersawn boards shrink 5% in width

Circles become ovals

Illus. 10-3. *Quartersawed boards shrink about half as much as plainsawed boards. They also have a tendency to stay flat and straight rather than cup and warp. For this reason, they are the ideal choice for the tops and bottoms of a box.*

their tendency to expand and contract. Quartersawed eastern white pine is the wood of choice for the tops and the bottoms because of its dimensional stability and workability (Illus. 10-3). Each growth ring in quartersawed boards is exposed, giving a uniform pattern of closely spaced lines. Hard maple and birch are nearly white in color and paint covers them easily. This was also a consideration when the original boxes were made, because the boxes were painted.

Two important concerns in selecting wood for these boxes are the grain direction and the moisture content of the wood. The bands must have straight grain running parallel to the surface. Selecting wood with grain that is not straight will greatly increase the chance of tear-out during the bending process. If possible, use air-dried lumber for the bands because it will bend more readily. Bands seem to work best when the wood that is used has been air-dried so that it has a moisture content of 14 to 18 percent. To minimize expansion and contraction for the tops and bottoms, use kiln-dried wood or wood that has been dried for a long time. The tops and bottoms should be dried to a moisture content of 8 to 9 percent to help prevent gaps from shrinkage or split board ends from expansion. Although pine, maple, and birch have been the traditional choices for boxes, a range of hardwoods is suitable for boxmaking; these woods include ash, cherry, walnut, and apple.

BOX-MAKING SUPPLIES AND INSTRUCTIONAL MATERIALS

Making oval boxes requires a number of supplies and tools. John Wilson, of the Home Shop, supplies Shaker box makers with a complete line of supplies and instructional materials. He teaches classes around the country in which people with little woodworking experience can make a set of five boxes in one day. The video *Making Shaker Oval Boxes with John Wilson* is very instructive. The class booklet used in his oval box workshops includes patterns for the five boxes as well as helpful directions. The Pattern Packet gives outlines and instructions for the entire line of boxes and carriers from the smallest #000 to #12. John Wilson also supplies material for bands, tops, and bottoms, as well as tacks, metal finger patterns, and forms. For a current price list of supplies and John Wilson's seminar schedule, write to John Wilson, The Home Shop, 500 East Broadway, Charlotte, Michigan 48813.

MAKING OVAL BOXES

Top and Bottom Wood

The pine tops and bottoms should be made from material long enough to pass safely through your planer. The tops for the #0 and #1 boxes are 3/16 inch thick. The tops for the #2, #3, #4, #5, and #6 boxes should be 1/4 inch thick. Local lumber stores usually have a source of 3/4-inch-thick pine material. Resaw the boards into halves and store them for a couple of weeks in a warm, dry space before thicknessing them to their final dimensions.

Cutting the Sides (Bands)

The most difficult part of preparing box stock is thicknessing band stock. The thickness of the bands, tops, and bottoms varies with each size box, as shown in Table 10-1. A band of the correct thickness will be able to bend around the oval form without breaking. Smaller boxes require thinner

BAND THICKNESS

Box number	Thickness × Width × Length of Wood	Top Band	Copper Tack	Top/Bottom Thickness	Oval
#0	.060" × 1 1/16" × 11 7/8"	7/16" × 12 1/4"	#1	3/16"	1 7/8" × 3 1/2"
#1	.062" × 1 1/2" × 15"	1/2" × 15 1/2"	#1	7/32"	2 9/16" × 4 9/16"
#2	.067" × 2" × 19"	5/8" × 19 3/4"	#1 1/2	1/4"	3 1/2" × 5 3/4"
#3	.072" × 2 1/2" × 23"	11/16" × 24"	#1 1/2	1/4"	4 1/2" × 7"
#4	.077" × 3 1/16" × 27"	3/4" × 28"	#2	1/4"	5 1/2" × 8 1/4"
#5	.085" × 3 11/16" × 31"	15/16" × 32"	#2	9/32"	6 1/2" × 9 1/2"
#6	.098" × 4 1/2" × 35 3/4"	1" × 37"	#2	5/16"	7 1/2" × 10 3/8"

Table 10-1.

bands to make the tighter-radius bends, but the larger boxes need the heft of the thicker veneers.

The thickness of veneer used will also depend on the copper tack sizes. The smaller copper tack, the #1 tack, will clinch two thicknesses of .060-inch veneer, but not veneer that is much thinner. The larger copper tack, the #2 tack, will clinch veneer .075 inch to .100 inch thick. The thickness of wood will depend on the species of the wood and the moisture content.

Once you've selected your stock, cut the bands. These must be very thin; the bands for the oval boxes shown in this chapter vary from just 1/16 inch thick for the three smaller boxes to 3/32 inch for the other four sizes of boxes. To make this thin stock, first rip the wood to the required band width; then resaw it on a band or table saw. Cut the wood slightly thicker than needed; then plane or sand it to its final thickness.

The box sides can be taken to final thickness with a hand scraper, hand plane, or sanding drum in a drill press. A dial caliper will give a very accurate dimension in thousandths of an inch.

Note: Make some extra band stock for each box. You may need it when it comes time to bend the wood.

Cutting the Fingers

To lay out the shape of the fingers, you will need a pattern. A thin piece of wood or Masonite™ will do. A more professional pattern can be made from aluminum available at a local lumberyard. This aluminum is prepainted white and cuts easily with shears or a utility knife. Mark where the copper tacks will be placed by drilling holes with a 5/64-inch drill bit.

Cut the band stock to the lengths you need. Lay out finger joints on one end of each band, as shown in Illus. 10-4. Then cut the fingers to shape with a band or a scroll saw. Drill the tack pilot holes with a 1/16-inch-diameter drill. Drilling the holes for the tacks will prevent the wood from splitting. If you want to produce several boxes of the same size, tape the band stock together and lay out the fingers on the top band; then saw and drill all the fingers simultaneously. Pick the end of the board with the straightest grain. Soaking the fingers in hot water softens the wood and makes it much easier to control the knife cut.

Start cutting at the base of each finger, making the bevel very steep—about 60 degrees. As you cut, decrease the angle of your knife (Illus. 10-5). By the time you get to the end of the finger, the angle of the bevel should be 30 degrees. Also cut a bevel on the very end of each finger. Be careful when cutting not to introduce any hairline cracks, which will expand during the bending process.

The final step in preparing the band stock for bending is to feather the end of the band opposite the fingers. Cut the box side to final length. In order to make as

Illus. 10-4. *Lay out the fingers on the ends of the board that has the straightest grain. This makes the cutting easier. (This photo and Illus. 10-5, 10-9–10-12, 10-16, 10-17, and 10-19–10-21 are courtesy of Charles Harvey, Berea, Kentucky.)*

Illus. 10-5. *To cut the fingers, use a sharp knife and begin the cut at the apex of the Gothic arch. Press the knife firmly and pull it with a sweeping motion. It may take more than one pass to cut all the way through. Take care not to introduce any hairline cracks because they'll get larger during the bending process.*

smooth a transition as possible from the inside of the box to the top where the band overlaps, it is necessary to taper the ends. Tapering the last 1 to 1½ inches of the band eliminates a bump inside the box where the band ends. You can taper the sides with a block plane or on a stationary belt sander using a wooden block to keep the band flat. The inside taper should be 1½ inches long, and taper to nearly 0 inch. Taper the inside of the fingers lightly.

Forms and Patterns

To make Shaker boxes, you need a few items. All of these items can also be purchased from John Wilson, of The Home Shop. You need two different forms. The box is bent around these forms, which ensure consistent shape and size. One form is the thick mould around which the band is bent, and the other form is the shaper that is pressed into both sides of the bands for drying (Illus. 10-6). The mould is a wooden oval as thick as the box is tall. The Shakers added metal anvils to allow the bending and clinching operation to take place at the same time. You can make your own forms from pine, basswood, or laminated plywood. If you intend to make several boxes, give the forms a coat of polyurethane. Cut the forms to a rough shape on the band saw and then sand them to the final shape on the disc or belt sander.

The shaper is put into both sides of the damp band to retain the shape of the band until it dries. Shapers are made of ¼- to

Illus. 10-6. *The band is bent around a mould, which is the thick piece of oval wood shown in the middle of this photo. The mould should be a little wider than the width of the band. The patterns on the left and on the right are for the top and bottom. The line on the patterns indicates the shape of the mould.*

¾-inch-thick material and have holes in them which allow air to pass through. As the shaper is pressed into the damp band, it can be adjusted so that it fits better. Make two shapers for each box. The shapers will be placed at the top and bottom edges of the drying side band (Illus. 10-7).

When making the shapers, use the same oval pattern used for the mould and then cut between ⅟₁₆ and ⅛ inch outside the line on a 10-degree bevel. Then sand up to the line with a stationary disc sander or belt sander with the table tilted at 10 degrees.

Illus. 10-7. *You will need some supplies to make the Shaker boxes. These supplies include a mould, which is shown on the upper left, and shapers, which are shown on the upper right. These two shapers are used to hold the shape of the wet band after it has been tacked. In the foreground are aluminum patterns for the top and bottom and the fingers.*

Bending and Tacking the Bands

The next step consists of soaking the bands in hot water before bending them around a form. Soaking the bands makes them pliable. This necessitates a tray long enough to hold the bands that is watertight and durable enough to withstand some time on a hot stove. A steel rain gutter with end caps soldered in place or connected with a heat-resistant epoxy putty works well. A painted, steel window planter tray is another option. A cover is needed to bring the temperature of the water up to 180 to 200 degrees Fahrenheit (83 to 94 degrees Celsius), and a piece of plywood will serve this purpose. If the water boils, it will not damage the wood. An electric hot plate is a good heat source (Illus. 10-8). Soak the bands for at least 20 minutes. When the bands are saturated, they will not float and soaking them any longer will be of no value.

Bending the bands takes some practice, and you should test the procedure a cou-

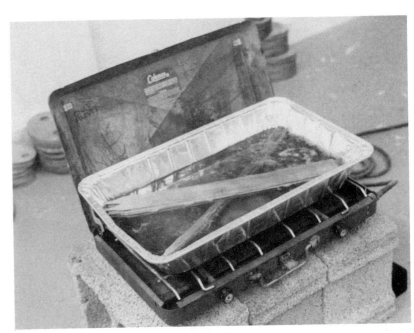

Illus. 10-8. *Heat the water for bending the bands on either a gas or an electric stove. If you use a gas stove, make sure that you have adequate ventilation. The water should be heated to roughly 200 degrees Fahrenheit (94 degrees Celsius).*

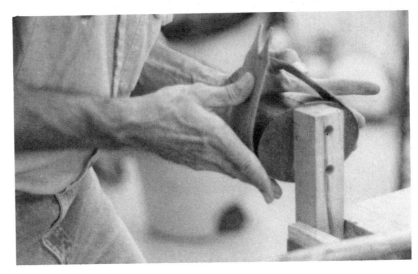

Illus. 10-9. *Work quickly when bending the band around the form. Try to do the bending in about 30 seconds or less. Be careful so that the area between the fingers doesn't split. If you can't get the bending done in this time frame, you can always resoak the band and try again.*

ple of times just to learn it. Get everything ready, so you can work quickly before the bands begin to cool. Try to get everything done in 25 to 35 seconds. If things do not go right, you can always resoak the bands.

Use tongs or some other device to pull a band out of the hot water and wrap it around the core (Illus. 10-9). Make sure to hold the fingers with both of the fingers supported, so that the band doesn't split. If one of the fingers is allowed to spring up, it might crack at the top of its arch.

Check to make sure that the bevelled side of the fingers faces out and that the tack line is aligned with the middle of the oval core. Place the tapered end of the band against the long side of the elliptical mould and wrap it as tightly as you can. Lap the fingers over the tapered end. The fingers must end up on the long side of the form, with their bevels facing out.

With the band wrapped around the core and the tack line centered on the core, draw a register mark across the top edges of the overlapped section at the front of the band. This mark will indicate where you should open the band to release the core and where to push the band back together so it forms the same size oval shaped on the core.

Carefully drive in the copper tacks that secure the fingers. You will need a way of bending the tacks. If you do not add anvils to the form you can use a piece of pipe secured in a vise or make a device with a pipe welded to it. Hammer and clinch the copper tacks at the same time by nailing them in over a pipe anvil, as shown in Illus. 10-10.

Next, take the top lid band out of the water and wrap it around the assembled bottom band. Then make the top band. Do this by repeating all the steps for the box band, except use the box band instead of a core to bend the top band. After tack-

ing the top band, slide it back on the box band to dry. Oval shapers pushed into the

Illus. 10-10. *If your forms do not have anvils, you can use a length of black pipe to cinch the tacks. This pipe is also useful for setting tacks that are not set completely the first time.*

top and bottom of the bands will maintain their shape.

Shapers are the oval discs (the same shape as the form) that are inserted after the tacks are clinched and the box is off the form. Although most box makers use two shapers with bevelled sides, an alternative is to use one shaper the size of the form and locate it in the middle of the box as shown in Illus. 10-11.

Leave the shaper or shapers in place for this operation. They shouldn't be in the way. Mark the location of the fingers on the top band and then tack it together in the same manner as the bottom band (Illus. 10-12). Put it back in place around the bottom band to dry. Adjust the top edge flush with the top of the bottom band, and turn it so all the fingers and tacks line up.

Soaking the band will raise the grain. When the box is dry, sand its inside. Sand-

Illus. 10-11. *Charles Harvey, who is a box maker in Berea, Kentucky, uses the single-spreader technique for making boxes.*

Illus. 10-12. *Cinch the tacks for the top band in a similar manner as the bottom band.*

ing the inside now is easy; you can sand the outside later. Let both bands dry for at least two days.

Fitting the Tops and Bottoms

The tops (lids) and bottoms of the traditional boxes were made of quartersawed pine. They are fitted dry and held in place with pegs. By not gluing the tops and the bottoms, they are free to expand and contract. The edges of the oval-shaped top and bottom are angled at a four- or five-degree angle and are pressed into the band (Illus. 10-13). Although the Shakers used pine, fancy woods may also be used as long as they are dry. Quartersawed material is ideal because it expands and contracts half as much as flatsawed material. This decreases the likelihood of breakage and cracks.

The bottom is usually fit first, and then

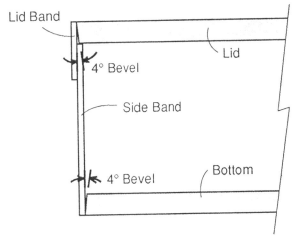

Illus. 10-13. *The top and the bottom are bevelled at a four-degree angle so that they can slide into the band with a tight fit.*

the top. Because it is so much easier to sand before the top and bottom are in place, do the sanding before assembly.

Mark the oval shape on the top or bottom using the dried bands or a mould (Illus. 10-14). Cut the outline on a band saw with the table tilted at four degrees (Illus. 10-15). The top and bottom should be slightly larger than their final sizes. The bottom patterns are the same as the core or inside oval. You have the option of using an oval pattern or the band itself. Each method is acceptable. A 2 percent enlargement of the bottom oval patterns shown in Illus. 10-22 is a close approximation, so it is important to cut outside the line. Top oval patterns are about ⅛ inch larger than bottom oval patterns.

Cutting and Sanding the Oval

This step consists of sanding the edges of the bottom and the band with the belt or disc sander table tilted at four degrees (Illus. 10-16). This sanding technique is used to shape the contour and to determine the final fit. First, establish the final edge

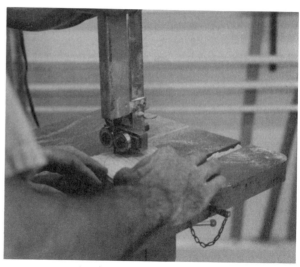

Illus. 10-15. *Using the band saw, cut about ¹/₁₆ inch outside the pencil line.*

Illus. 10-16. *Using a belt or a disc sander, refine the curve and get one long side of the top or bottom to fit into the bands.*

Illus. 10-14. *Using the dried band with the spreader in place as a template, draw the shape on the top and the bottom.*

shape and the bevel around the piece; don't sand up to the line yet. The idea is to make the bottom so that it fits tightly into the bands. The 4-degree bevel on the edge stretches the band, making the joint tight all around the circumference. With a pencil, mark one of the ends of the band and the bottom so that you can avoid confusion. It is better to sand slowly and test the fit several times. Take a little bit off at a

116

time and keep test-fitting. Sand half a perimeter at a time and get one side to fit first.

Before sanding the edges of the bottom and the band, choose which side of the band will be used; this decision will affect the finger direction of a box. The majority of the boxes have fingers pointing to the right, although left-pointing fingers are not uncommon. Top-band fingers always point in the same direction as the bottom-band fingers.

Press the bottom into place until the entire rim of the band is slightly above the surface (Illus. 10-17). Be careful not to put too much force on the fingers. It is better to have the pieces of the box fit too loosely than too tightly. If there is a gap, you can fill it with glue and then sand it. The sawdust will adhere to the glue and fill the gap. After assembly, sand the tops and bottoms flat on the belt sander.

After the bottom is fitted into the box band, the top band is placed back over the top of the bottom band and the top is marked and cut in a similar process as the bottom. However, another consideration is the fit between the assembled top and the completed bottom. Although a tight-fitting box can only be adjusted by removing material, a sloppy fit of a top band may

Illus. 10-17. *Using your fingers to test the fit, press the top and bottom gently together. Be careful not to apply so much pressure that the band deforms or breaks.*

be adjusted by changing the shape of the top oval.

The bottom is held in place with wooden pegs driven into predrilled pilot holes around the circumference of the box. Round toothpicks are perfect for this task (Illus. 10-18). Adjust the drill-press table so that it is parallel to the drill bit (Illus. 10-19). Using a $\frac{1}{16}$-inch bit, drill eight equally spaced holes $\frac{3}{8}$ inches deep into the top and bottom. Avoid drilling any

Illus. 10-18. *The tops and bottoms are not glued in place. They are held in place with wood pegs. Round toothpicks are perfect for this task. If you're going to make a number of boxes, it is best if you actually cut the box and toothpicks in half on a band saw.*

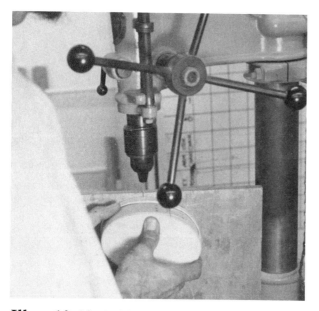

Illus. 10-19. *With the drill-press table tilted so that it is parallel to the bit, make eight holes around the box using a 1/16-inch bit.*

holes at the points of the oval where the curve makes the tightest bend, because the wood is under a lot of tension at that point and the band could crack or break.

Cut the toothpicks in half. Wipe the pointed end of the toothpick in glue and tap it into the hole as shown in Illus. 10-20. Avoid driving it in so far that the box side splits. Let the glue dry. Finish the process by snipping it off with pliers and levelling the remaining bit with a sharp chisel, utility knife, or sandpaper, depending on your taste and skill level (Illus. 10-21).

The Shakers painted their boxes up until the Civil War period; then they started using varnish. Modern box makers use a variety of paint, milk paint oil, or clear finishes. Sand the top and bottom as you would before applying any finish.

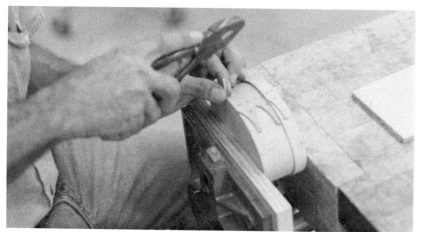

Illus. 10-20. *Put glue on the end of the toothpick and tap it into the box. Be careful not to split the wood.*

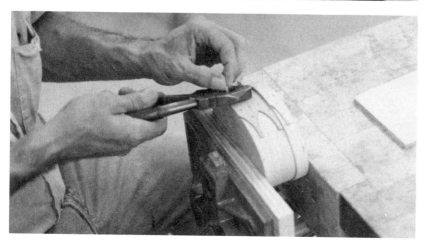

Illus. 10-21. *Using pliers, snip off the toothpick.*

118

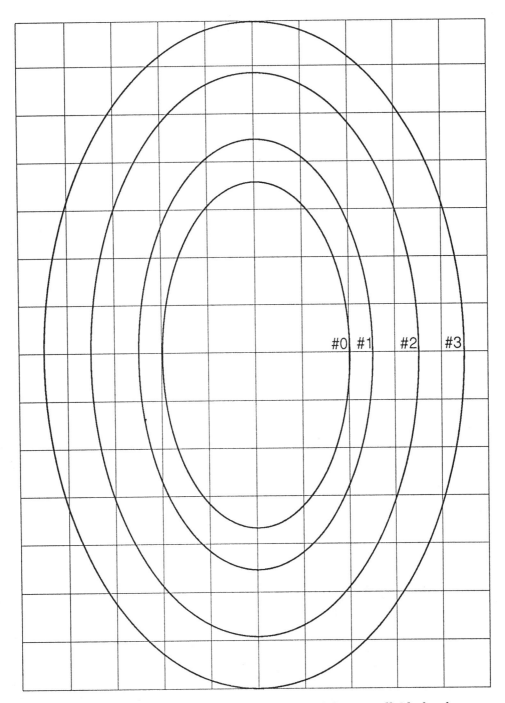

Within the figure: #0 #1 #2 #3

Illus. 10-22. *This drawing is the mould size of four small Shaker boxes. Each block is ½ inch.*

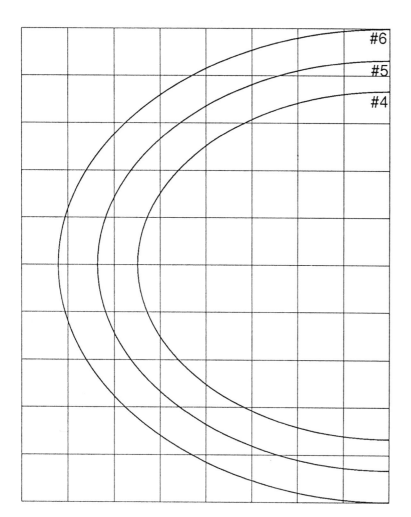

#6
#5
#4

Illus. 10-23. *This is a half-pattern for the largest three Shaker boxes. Each block is ½ inch.*

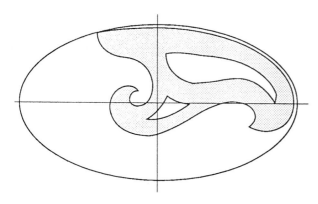

Illus. 10-24. *A French curve is useful for laying out the shape of the oval.*

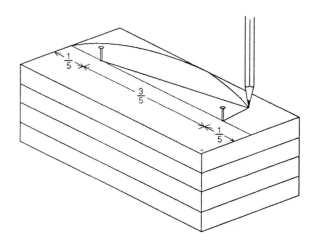

Illus. 10-25. *A string and nails are also useful for laying out the shape of the oval.*

Illus. 10-26. *The shape of the oval can also be laid out using a number of points on two axes.*

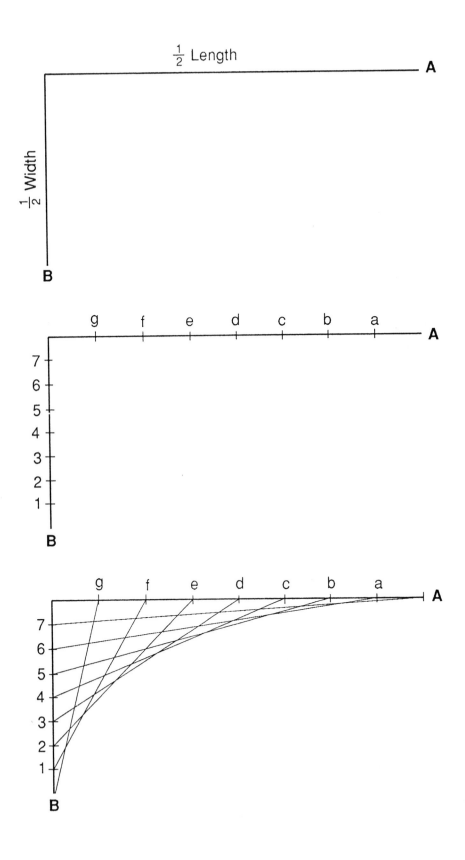

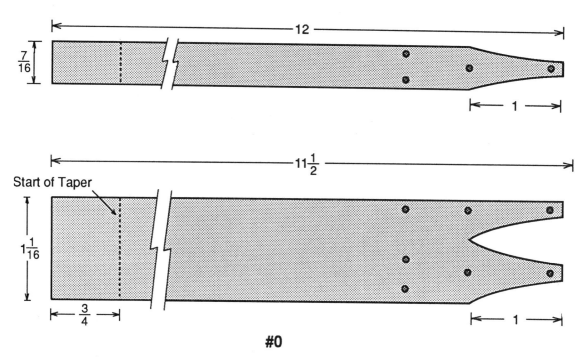

#0

Illus. 10-27. *Band pattern for the #0 box. The band is .060 inch thick.*

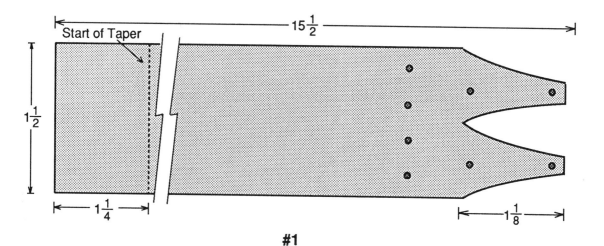

#1

Illus. 10-28. *Pattern for the #1 box. The band is .062 inch thick.*

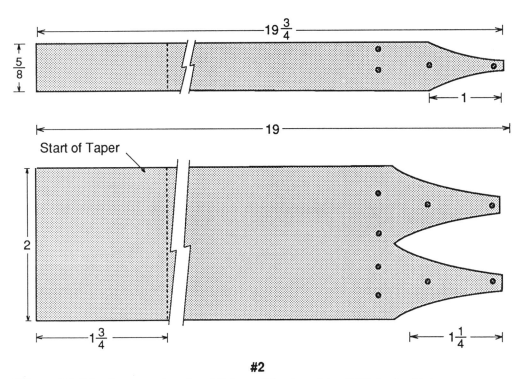

Illus. 10-29. *Pattern for the #2 box. The band is .067 inch thick.*

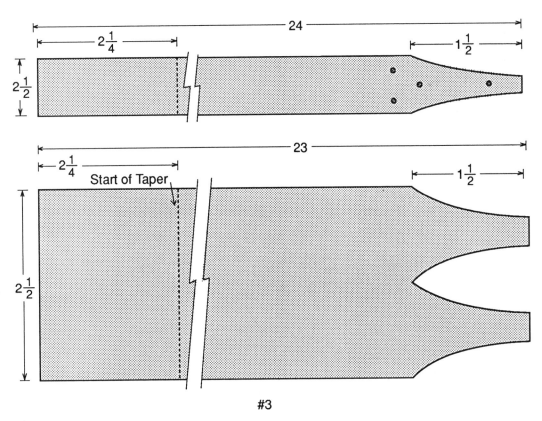

Illus. 10-30. *Pattern for the #3 box. The band is .072 inch thick.*

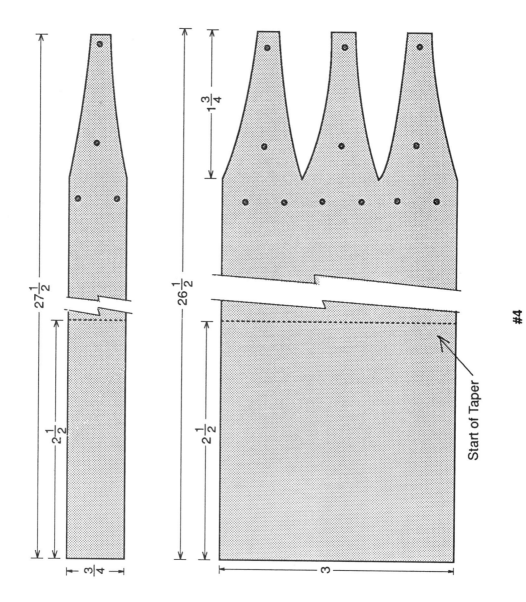

Illus. 10-31. *Pattern for the #4 box. The band is .077 inch thick.*

#4

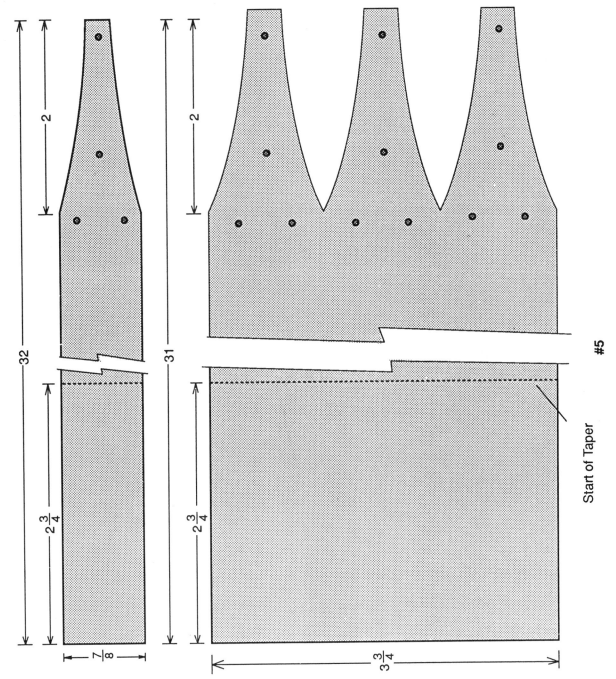

Illus. 10-32. *The pattern for the #5 box. This band should be .085 inch thick.*

#5

Start of Taper

125

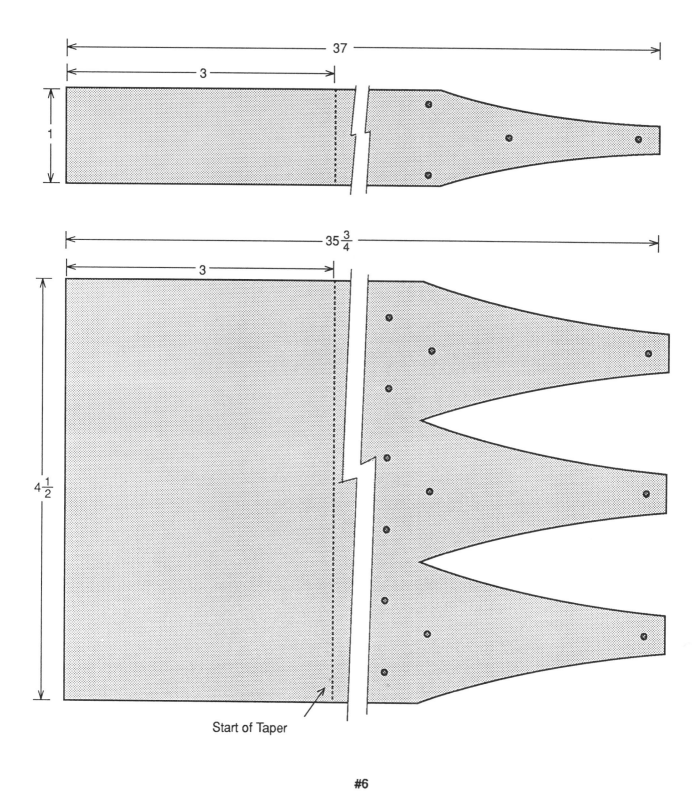

#6

Illus. 10-33. *This is the pattern for the largest Shaker box, which is #6. The band should be .095 inch thick.*

MISCELLANEOUS PROJECTS

Illus. 10-34–10-49 feature plans and details for making other Shaker projects in which steam-bending techniques are used. These projects include carrier trays, wood scoops, and circular wall sconces.

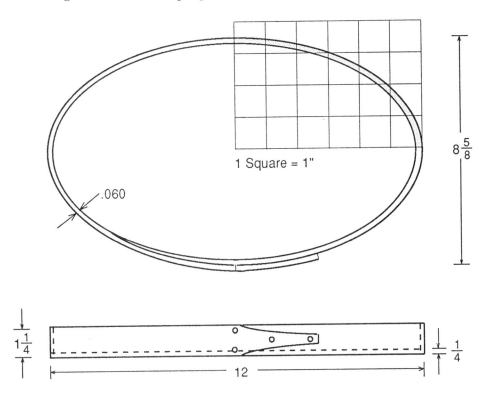

1 Square = 1"

.060

$8\frac{5}{8}$

$1\frac{1}{4}$

$\frac{1}{4}$

12

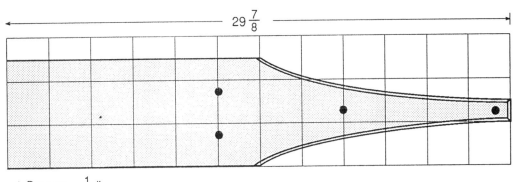

$29\frac{7}{8}$

1 Square = $\frac{1}{2}$"

Illus. 10-34. *Pattern for the simple tray shown in Illus 10-35.*

Illus. 10-35. *This tray is a good first bending project. It has a very simple design: It has only two pieces of wood and one finger.*

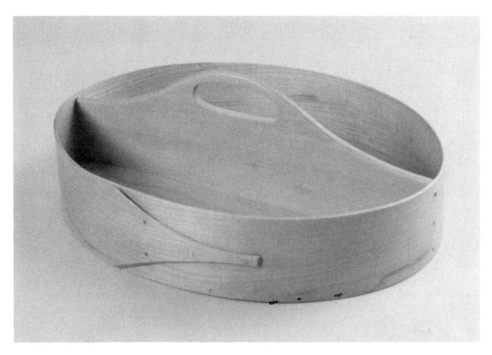

Illus. 10-36. *A carrier tray, which also has a very simple design. It is similar to the tray shown in Illus. 10-35 except that a piece of wood is added to the middle.*

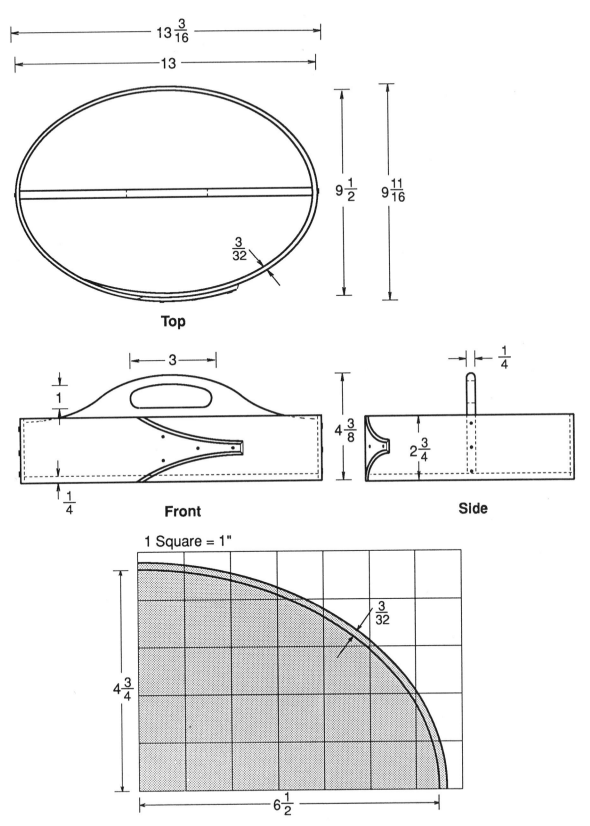

Illus. 10-37. *Plan for the carrier tray shown in Illus. 10-36.*

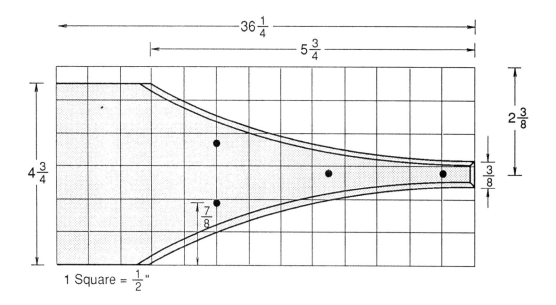

1 Square = $\frac{1}{2}$"

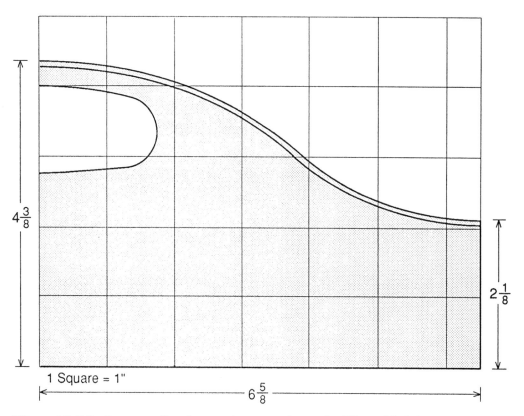

1 Square = 1"

Illus. 10-38. *Patterns for the carrier tray shown in Illus. 10-36.*

Illus. 10-39. *Tray with bent-wood handle. See Illus. 10–41 and 10-42 for details and plans.*

Illus. 10-40. *Small carrier with bent-wood handles. See Illus. 10-43 and 10-44 for details and plans.*

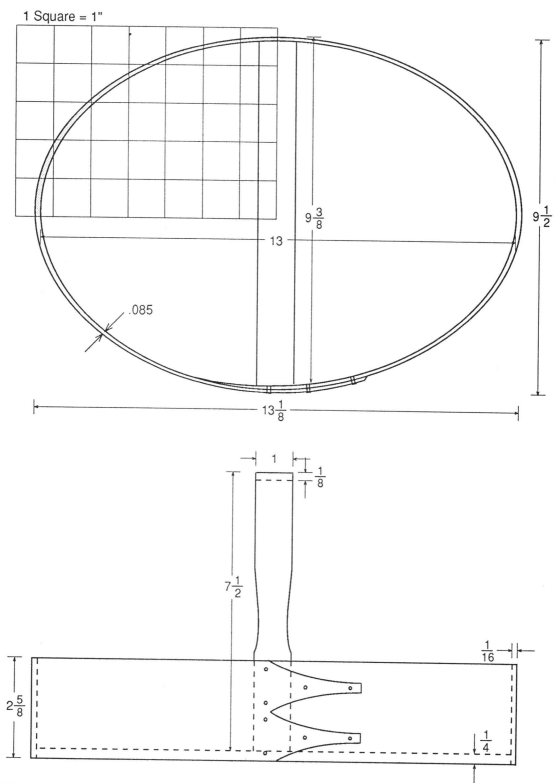

Illus. 10-41. *Plan for the tray shown in Illus. 10-39.*

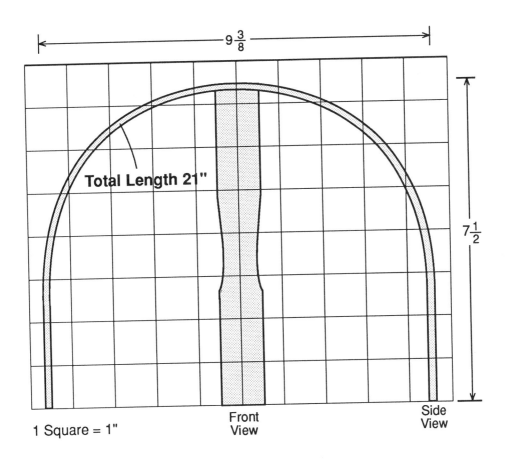

Total Length 21"

9 3/8

7 1/2

1 Square = 1"

Front
View

Side
View

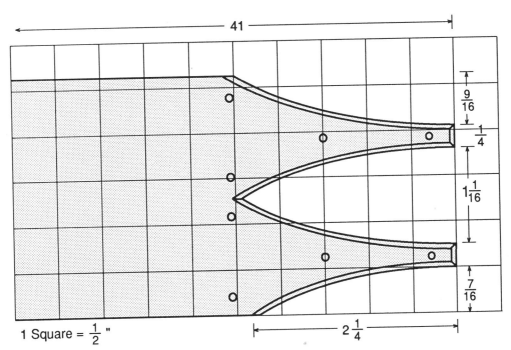

41

9/16

1/4

1 1/16

7/16

1 Square = 1/2 "

2 1/4

Illus. 10-42. *Details of band and carrier handle for the tray shown in Illus. 10-39.*

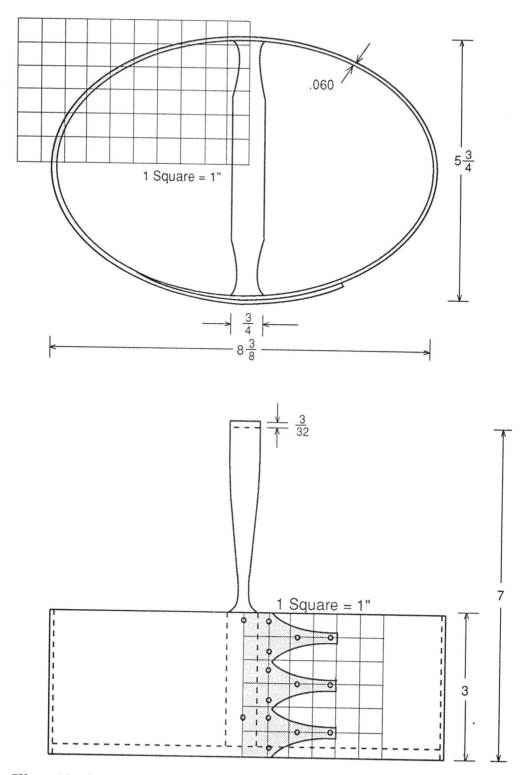

.060

5 $\frac{3}{4}$

1 Square = 1"

$\frac{3}{4}$

8 $\frac{3}{8}$

$\frac{3}{32}$

1 Square = 1"

7

3

Illus. 10-43. *Plan for the small carrier with the bent-wood handle.*

Illus. 10-44.
Detail of handle for the carrier shown in Illus. 10-40.

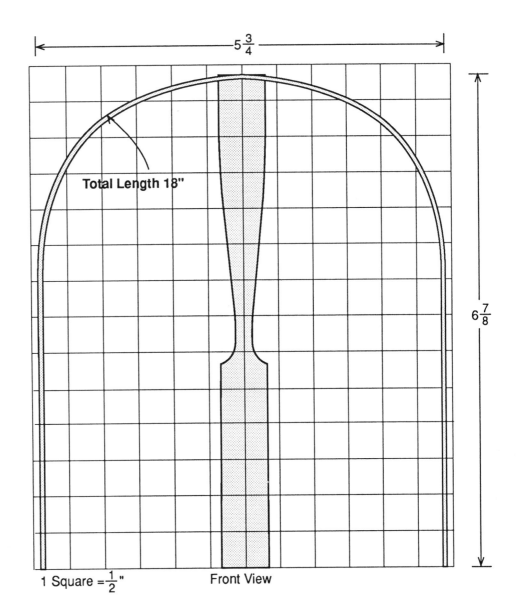

5 ¾

Total Length 18"

6 ⅞

1 Square = ½"

Front View

Illus. 10-45. *Bent-wood scoop. Before the days of metal and plastic scoops, wood scoops were very popular. This one features a turned handle.*

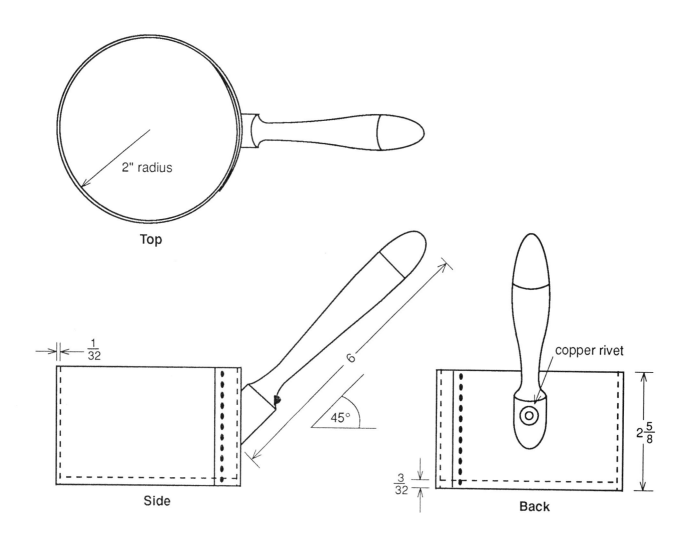

Top

$\frac{1}{32}$

Side

6

45°

Back

copper rivet

$2\frac{5}{8}$

$\frac{3}{32}$

2" radius

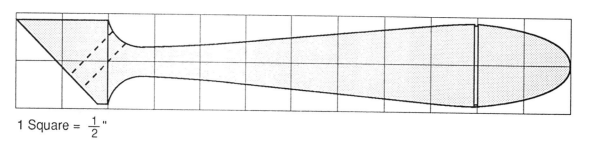

1 Square = $\frac{1}{2}$"

Illus. 10-46. *Plan for the bent-wood scoop shown in Illus. 10-45.*

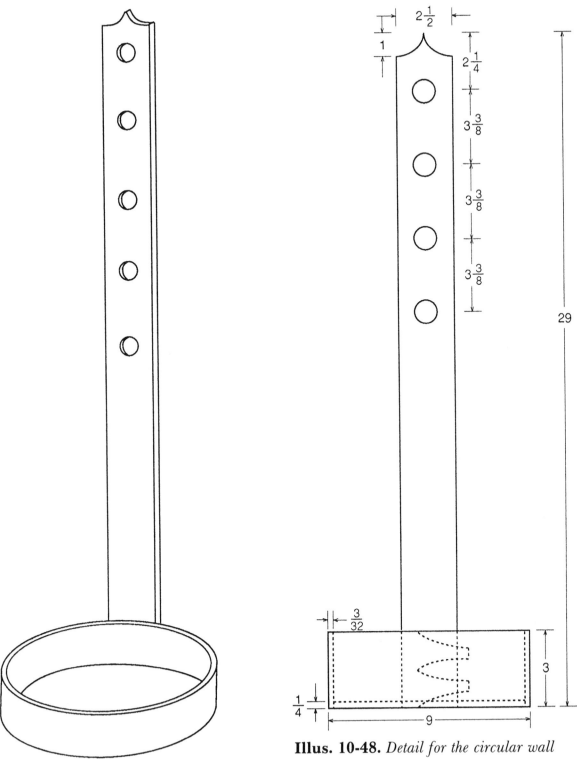

Illus. 10-47. *Circular wall sconce.*

Illus. 10-48. *Detail for the circular wall sconce.*

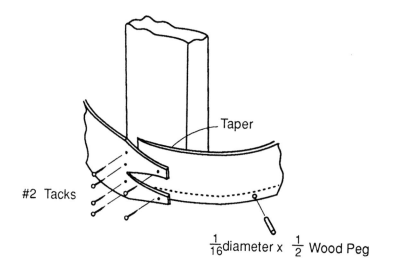

Taper

#2 Tacks

$\frac{1}{16}$ diameter x $\frac{1}{2}$ Wood Peg

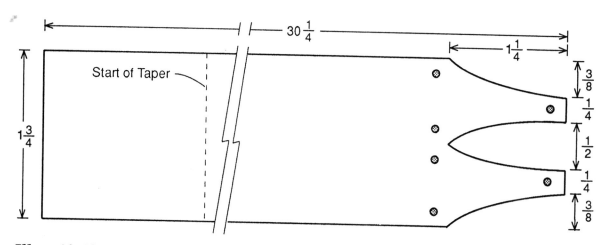

Start of Taper

$30\frac{1}{4}$

$1\frac{1}{4}$

$1\frac{3}{4}$

$\frac{3}{8}$

$\frac{1}{4}$

$\frac{1}{2}$

$\frac{1}{4}$

$\frac{3}{8}$

Illus. 10-49. *Detail for construction of the circular wall sconce.*

Appendices

❖ ❖ ❖

A Guide to Shaker Sites and Collections

THERE ARE EIGHT remaining Shaker communities that are open to the public. Some villages have been completely restored, while work actively continues on others. Despite the degree of restoration, the graceful proportions of the buildings, the sense of industry and purpose, and the subtle beauty of the workmanship never ceases to work its magic on the visitor. Shaker artifacts are also found elsewhere in various collections and museums.

ORIGINAL SHAKER VILLAGES

Mt. Lebanon Shaker Village
Shaker Road
New Lebanon, New York 12125
(518) 794-9500

Watervliet Shaker Site
Shaker Heritage Society
1848 Shaker Meeting House
Albany Shaker Road
Albany, New York 12211
(518) 456-7890

Hancock Shaker Village
P.O. Box 898
Pittsfield, Massachusetts 01202
(413) 443-0188

Enfield Shaker Village Museum
Enfield, New Hampshire 03748
(603) 632-5533

Canterbury Shaker Village
Canterbury, New Hampshire 03224
(603) 783-9977

Sabbath Day Lake
The United Society of Shakers
Poland Spring, Maine 04274
(207) 926-4391

Shakertown at Pleasant Hill
3501 Lexington Road
Harrodsburg, Kentucky 40330
(606) 734-5411

Shakertown at South Union
Highway 68-80
Post Office Box 30
South Union, Kentucky 42283
(502) 542-4167

COLLECTIONS

Fruitland Museum
Prospect Hill
Harvard, Massachusetts 01451
(617) 456-3924

Metric Equivalents

INCHES TO MILLIMETRES AND CENTIMETRES

MM—millimetres   CM—centimetres

Inches	MM	CM	Inches	CM	Inches	CM
⅛	3	0.3	9	22.9	30	76.2
¼	6	0.6	10	25.4	31	78.7
⅜	10	1.0	11	27.9	32	81.3
½	13	1.3	12	30.5	33	83.8
⅝	16	1.6	13	33.0	34	86.4
¾	19	1.9	14	35.6	35	88.9
⅞	22	2.2	15	38.1	36	91.4
1	25	2.5	16	40.6	37	94.0
1¼	32	3.2	17	43.2	38	96.5
1½	38	3.8	18	45.7	39	99.1
1¾	44	4.4	19	48.3	40	101.6
2	51	5.1	20	50.8	41	104.1
2½	64	6.4	21	53.3	42	106.7
2	76	7.6	22	55.9	43	109.2
3½	89	8.9	23	58.4	44	111.8
4	102	10.2	24	61.0	45	114.3
4½	114	11.4	25	63.5	46	116.8
5	127	12.7	26	66.0	47	119.4
6	152	15.2	27	68.6	48	121.9
7	178	17.8	28	71.1	49	124.5
8	203	20.3	29	73.7	50	127.0

ACKNOWLEDGMENTS

Thanks to the following people for their help:

Kate Morris

Jenny Wilcox, for her drawings

Marcheta Sparrow and Larrie Spier Curry, Pleasant Hill, Kentucky

Jerry Grant, from the Shaker Museum at Old Chatham, New York

Seth Reed, the resident cabinetmaker at Hancock Shaker Village, in Massachusetts

Charles Harvey, Berea, Kentucky

John Wilson, Charlotte, Michigan

Index